Silver Link Silk Editions

SLP

Enjoying the Cumbrian Coast Railway

David John Hindle MA

Silver Link Silk Editions

SLP

Enjoying the Cumbrian Coast Railway

David John Hindle MA

Silver Link Publishing Ltd

Contents

First published in 2017

British Library Cataloguing in Publication Data

A catalogue record for this book is available from the British Library.

ISBN 978 1 85794 497 6

Silver Link Publishing Ltd
The Trundle
Ringstead Road
Great Addington
Kettering
Northants NN14 4BW
Tel/Fax: 01536 330588
email: sales@nostalgiacollection.com
Website: www.nostalgiacollection.com

Printed and bound in the Czech Republic

Half title: Representing those great days of steam is this stunning photograph of the *Flying Scotsman* crossing Arnside Viaduct with a northbound special in May, 1990. *Peter Fitton*

Dedicated to my late grandparents Roland Bowman and his wife Winifrid Jane Bloomfontein Bowman who first introduced me to the Cumbrian Coast Railway

Foreword

By Lord Horam of Grimsargh in the County of Lancashire

David Hindle is a social historian of infectious enthusiasm and rare skill. He has already immortalised the village of my birth in *Grimsargh, the story of a Lancashire village* and encapsulated the enjoyment of aspects of a life in Preston in *Twice Nightly: An illustrated history of entertainment in Preston.* Now he sets out to capture the enjoyment brought to thousands by the Cumbrian Coastal Line.

This is a remarkable local story. These days people go to the Lake District for its stunning scenery, but in the Victorian era the beautiful Eskdale Valley and Furness areas were a centre of mining and manufacturing. The Cumbrian Coastal Line was conceived originally to assist with the extraction of iron ore and coal and the manufacture of steel products. But local industrialists even then foresaw the potential for carrying passengers as well as freight.

The coastal railway line from Carnforth to Barrow remains as a vital artery to an important town. The section from Barrow up the Cumbrian coast to Whitehaven faced the 'Beeching axe' in the 1960s. It was saved by determined local effort. This significant railway was crucial for the well-being of the many small towns and villages strung along the coast but, as David shows, it has also become a source of enjoyment and pleasure to thousands. Railway buffs, fell-walkers, cyclists, photographers, naturalists and birdwatchers, as well as ordinary holidaymakers, all use the services regularly. The historic narrow-gauge steam railway from Ravenglass to Dalegarth continues to convey tourists into the Eskdale valley.

Resurrected diesel locomotives power some of the regular services between Carnforth and Carlisle, but there are steam train excursions on the line and it has even had the privilege of hosting several journeys by the famous *Flying Scotsman*. In true Wainwright style, David also describes several local scenic walks starting from stations along the line.

Writing about the enjoyment and pleasure afforded by this railway and local facilities, as well as their history, is a novel concept. David Hindle brings it off triumphantly, and all who love the Lakes will enjoy this book.

John Horam

Acknowledgements

I am very grateful for the help and encouragement of Aidan Turner Bishop; Peter Fitton, for his excellent photographs of steam and diesel locomotives; Mark Bartlett, for providing a brilliant selection of photographs of diesel locomotives at short notice; Peter Smith and Geoff Carefoot, for superb photographs of British birds and wildlife; David Eaves, for his unstinting technical help and exquisite artistry of Furness Railway locomotives, photographs and humorous caricatures; and Peter Van Zeller (Curator and revered driver) and David Rounce (Manager) of the Ravenglass Railway Museum, for all their valuable help with the history of the Ravenglass & Eskdale Railway, and for supplying some rare and historic photographs of 'The Ratty' throughout the ages. The Bob Gregson railway archive for historic images and ephemera.

Research has encompassed a wide range of primary sources. I acknowledge the help of staff at the National Archive, Kew, London; National Railway Museum, York; Cumbrian Railways Association, Harris Reference Library, Preston; and Lancashire, Barrow, Kendal and Carlisle County Record Offices. Thanks also to journalists of long ago who wrote in local newspapers about the social impact of railways on local communities. I thank all contributors, while pointing out that I have made every effort to trace copyright owners of material and apologise for possible omissions.

Introduction

I have always been fascinated by railways, especially by the magic of the steam era, the journey itself, and in particular the social history of the Furness Railway and its associated branch lines. The earliest railways acted as a catalyst for population growth and the expansion of the country's towns and villages. The line serving Furness and the Cumbrian Coast was no exception, substantially contributing to the creation of a new industrialised working class and rapid population growth. It has also always been inextricably linked with the local economy, fulfilling both social and economic needs. Since 1857 it has provided a considerably more direct route than road to the coastal towns of Grange-over-Sands, Ulverston, Barrow-in-Furness and the Cumbrian coast by skirting Morecambe Bay.

This fascinating and historic railway threads its way along the peripheral areas of the Lake District and the West Cumbrian coast. Undeniably the way that the 'Cumbrian Coast Line' embraces the coast is one of its most pleasing characteristics

with ever-changing scenery from Morecambe Bay to the Solway Plain.

It is essentially a rural railway, yet brimming with the nostalgia of a bygone age and not unlike the branch lines of times gone by. At times I believe it to be in a time warp that

Class 31 Nos 31130 *Calder Hall Power Station* and 31304, with a train of nuclear flasks from Valley, Anglesey, to Sellafield, are seen here at Meathop near Grange on 16 April 1984. *Peter Fitton*

amazingly survived the interventions of Dr Richard Beeching during the 1960s. However, a prime factor for retention was its important role in the transportation of nuclear waste to the remotely situated Sellafield nuclear fuel reprocessing and decommissions plant, whose reliance on the railway is vital to the nuclear industry. Calder Hall Power Station and the adjoining Windscale Nuclear Reprocessing Plant opened in 1953, providing a significant economic and employment boost for West Cumberland, but owing to a disastrous fire in 1957 the plant has since been named Sellafield.

The focus of this book is the core route of the original Furness Railway from Carnforth to Barrow-in-Furness, Millom and Whitehaven. The line retains the title Furness Railway from Carnforth to Barrow-in-Furness and serves a number of Victorian resorts and small towns, principally Silverdale, Arnside, Grange-over-Sands, Ulverston and Dalton-in-Furness. North of Barrow-in-Furness the meandering and captivating route to Millom, Whitehaven, Workington and Carlisle

is today aptly named the Cumbrian Coast Line.

Overall, *Enjoying the Cumbrian Coast Line* is designed to appeal to lovers of the Lake District and its awesome countryside as well as tourists, railway historians and enthusiasts, photographers, hikers, cyclists, naturalists and in particular ornithologists. With regard to the latter category, I believe there is a Freudian link for many people between railways and those who have a penchant for the popular hobby of birdwatching that is tucked away in one's psyche. I have actually known many devotees of both pursuits, most of whom

like to observe, record and classify.

Although there is a general acceptance by all that the wonderful days of steam have irrevocably gone, there is still a yearning for unashamed nostalgia. Accordingly a reawakening of memories is captured with a photographic portfolio of steam and diesel locomotives at work on the Furness Line throughout the book.

I grew up with this railway and clearly my affection for it remains to this day. In my opinion the history and scenic grandeur of this line have been far too long overlooked. Therefore, my principal aim is to redress and raise the profile of

Class 4F No 44157 and hoppers pass Workington Main No 2 on 13 June 1964. *Peter Fitton*

this railway line by focussing on its increasing use for pleasure from the Victorian era to the present day. I include information about the social and economic history of the area it serves and anecdotes from people associated with the line.

During Cumbria's industrial revolution, iron ore extraction and steel manufacture were the dominant industries in towns such as Barrow-in-Furness, Workington and Millom. The Furness Railway Company was conceived in 1843 to exploit the recently discovered iron ore and slate deposits at Dalton and Kirkby-in-Furness, and it opened with a mineral line in 1846, linking Furness with the sea at Piel Port on the south-west tip of the Furness peninsula. Consistent with national trends, the earliest railway gradually linked up with other routes, thus providing increased capacity for iron ore, coal and sundry traffic. Simultaneously local tycoons and industrialists foresaw its potential for carrying passengers as well as freight.

The Cumbrian Coastal route evolved from piecemeal railway construction and consolidation along the coast by

five different railway companies, which began in 1845 and was completed in 1857. These independent companies were: 1) the Maryport & Carlisle, opening in 1845; 2) the Furness Railway, opening in 1846; 3) the Whitehaven Junction Railway, connecting Whitehaven with Maryport in 1847; 4) the Whitehaven & Furness Junction Railway, opening in 1850; and 5) the Ulverston & Lancaster Railway, completed in 1857.

Thus by 1857 the Furness Railway had evolved to serve West Cumberland and the

Above: Class 47 No 47445 crosses the imposing Arnside Viaduct with the 16.30 Barrow to Preston train on 25 August 1989. *Peter Fitton*

Left: Class 31 No 31232 powers the 14.48 Manchester Victoria to Barrow train on 10 September 1990. A clue to the location is clearly revealed. *Peter Fitton*

emerging railway network. It was connected with the main Lancaster & Carlisle Railway to the south at Carnforth and with the Whitehaven Junction Railway to the north. These two companies were both taken over by the London & North Western Railway (LNWR) in 1866, while the Maryport & Carlisle remained independent until the 1923 Grouping.

I believe that knowledge of the line's heritage will enrich enjoyment and make travel more interesting, for there is plenty to observe along the route, including relics of industrial archaeology, which can best be observed and understood from the train. Accordingly I begin with a concise social history of the Furness Railway in Chapter 1.

The coming of the first railways revolutionised travel, and excursion traffic began the mass market for leisure. In the mid-19th century the celebrated poet William Wordsworth expressed doubts about railways being compatible with the history and beauty of England's glorious Lake District. Chapters 2 and 3 tell the story of how Wordsworth's Lakeland was about to change with mass tourism during the mid- to late-Victorian era, brought there by the national and Furness Railway network. I illustrate how the Victorians enjoyed the Furness Railway, with combined ship, train and charabanc tours

Trainloads of Edwardian holidaymakers arrive at Blackpool Central station, some of whom were probably about to discover Lakeland for the first time with a combined tour over the Furness Railway. *Bob Gregson railway archive*

penetrating Lakeland, especially during the annual Wakes Weeks. These were factors that led to a burgeoning Furness Railway and the established Lakeland tourist industry, despite Wordsworth's disapproval.

In Chapter 4 I draw on a range of interests, including those passengers who simply enjoy a scenic and nostalgic train

ride and for whom I offer some guidance to features to be observed along the line. Where appropriate, references to items of cultural and historic interest have been incorporated.

Chapter 5 embraces a potpourri of information and memories that have stimulated research and provided the inspiration to share a measure of the charm and magnetism of the railway and its branches. I reminisce about holidays spent during the wakes, including travelling along the Lakeland branch lines with a holiday Runabout ticket. In those pre-Beeching days before there were massive cuts to the railways, local and primitive branch lines like those to Coniston and Lakeside impacted on the lives of the first railway passengers.

Chapter 6 features exquisite and wonderful drawings of the various classes of Furness Railway locomotives compiled by my old friend David Eaves. In Chapter 7 I look at 20th-century developments and the demise of steam, which heralded the preservation movement. Steam excursions along the Cumbrian coast during the second half of the 20th and into the 21st century are a fine example of how the Furness Line is nowadays used for pleasure. Chapters 8 and 9 look at the role of excursions trains, harking back over two centuries of steam locomotion and excursions on the Furness Line and its branches.

In complete contrast to the steam giants of yesteryear, the diminutive Ravenglass & Eskdale narrow-gauge steam railway is described in Chapter 10. A portfolio of unique photographs illustrates the origins of this fascinating railway and how it too has been used for pleasure since the Victorians first discovered the delights of the Eskdale valley. So why not journey with me behind

Class 47 No 47186 (shedded at Tinsley) calls at Grange on 23 May 1982 with the 09.00 service from Barrow to Manchester Victoria. *Peter Fitton*

Ivatt Class 4MT 2-6-0s Nos 43025 and 43006 stand outside Workington MPD on 13 June 1964. *Peter Fitton*

a gleaming veteran steam engine on the affectionately named 'La'al Ratty'? A guide to the line and the wildlife to be observed from it features in Chapter 11.

For cyclists, participating stations offer an affordable and flexible bike hire scheme to explore the Lake District. Cyclists can meander along the country lanes of Lakeland or seek a range of forest trails in Whinlatter Forest ranging from the single-track Altura Trail to the less vigorous forest roads and bridleways.

Chapter 12 brings the Furness and Cumbrian Coast lines up to date. Today the modern railway continues to satisfy the needs of the travelling public, and is also increasingly being used for pleasure with a range of day ticket options valid within a defined area. In this chapter I also explain how resurrected diesel locomotives working service trains have become celebrities in their own right.

Taken as a whole, the area covered by this book is indisputably a great region in which to enjoy fantastic scenery combined with the great birdwatching and heritage walks.

In Chapter 13 I detail eight scenic walks with a focus on natural history and ornithological interest and, where appropriate, their historic features and associated railway heritage. The walks have been selected to appeal to solo walkers as well as families, birdwatchers and those with an eclectic range of interests.

The Furness Railway and its branch lines led to a transport revolution, affording ordinary people greater mobility for work, business and pleasure. Excursion trains, steam specials and regular services have enriched the lives of rail passengers throughout two centuries of rail travel. Accordingly, it may be contended that passengers have come to regard the railway journey along the Cumbrian Coast as one of Britain's great railway journeys. For me it has been an edifying experience and I have come to regard it simply as a railway for pleasure, taking me in the right direction to interesting and thought-provoking places along the Cumbrian Coast and the much-loved English Lake District.

Far left: A striking image of No 790 *Hardwicke* (built 1892, LMS No 5031, withdrawn in 1932) leaving Grange for Carnforth in May 1976. It may now been seen at the National Railway Museum. *Peter Fitton*

Left: An early visit to Ravenglass by David Hindle. *David Hindle*

Right: The 10.04 Preston to Barrow train, diagrammed for Class 37 haulage, awaits departure from Preston station in June 2016. *Graham Wilkinson*

Far right: It is possible to see the red squirrel and the otter in the Lake District and around Morecambe Bay. *Both Peter Smith*

Below: River Mite is turned at Ravenglass. *David Hindle*

1 A concise history of the Furness Railway

The historic background to the line should help to stimulate further interest for passengers enjoying a journey along it. The Furness Railway was originally conceived as a mineral railway for the carriage of coal, iron ore and slates, and was integrated as part of a grandiose scheme to link England with Scotland.

At Whitehaven coal-mining was the dominant industry, and next to the sea the King Pit shaft was sunk in 1750. It reached a depth of 160 fathoms and at the time the mine was considered to be the deepest in the world. Coal mines were dangerous places but a necessary evil to put food on the table. The coal industry was alluded to by Daniel Defoe while visiting the town in 1725:

'Whitehaven has grown up from a small place to be considerable by the coal trade, which increased to be very considerable of late, that it is now the most common part of England for shipping off coal except Newcastle and Sunderland.'

In 1785 the main route to reach the area was across the treacherous sands of Morecambe Bay by stagecoach. Thereafter came the canal era and the unique Ulverston Canal, which was constructed in 1796.

At the tip of the Furness peninsula lies Barrow-in-Furness. In 1805 it was described as 'the hamlet of Barrow with a small sea port situated about three miles south west of Furness Abbey.' Prior to the coming of the railway Furness was very isolated, with a small population of 130 in the early 19th century, but in less than half a century the settlement was transformed from a village to a town with a population of 60,000.

Tracking the growth of the Furness Railway and its central protagonists

The stagecoach and other methods of transportation were soon to be superseded by the railways. In 1820 there were no commercial passenger railways in Britain, but by 1912 the landscape had been transformed, with 120 companies operating more than 20,000 miles of track. In West Cumbria alone up to seven different railway companies were in operation prior to completion of the established Furness Railway in 1857.

The route from Carnforth to Carlisle began with the emergence of the Maryport & Carlisle Railway in 1845. North of Whitehaven, the line reached Carlisle by 1847 by means of the Whitehaven Junction Railway (to Maryport) and the Maryport & Carlisle Railway (on to Carlisle). Neither of the companies operating these lines ever formed part of the original Furness Railway.

In 1837 the great railway engineer George Stephenson formulated a planned extension of his Maryport & Carlisle Railway, then under construction to Lancaster. The ambitious proposal would have crossed the Duddon estuary on a mile-long viaduct and Morecambe Bay by means of an 11-mile embankment and viaducts. The cost of the two crossings was put at £362,861 for Morecambe Bay and £71,270 for the Duddon estuary. As time went by it was found impossible to raise the money and the plan was abandoned on 21 April 1838.

Despite rejection of this the grandest of schemes, following an agreement with the Earl of Lonsdale George Stephenson became the engineer in charge of construction of the Whitehaven & Furness Junction Railway. This line reached Broughton-in-Furness in 1850, connecting with the evolving Furness Railway and Barrow-in-Furness to the south.

The original Furness Railway played a pivotal role in developing Barrow's iron and steel manufacturing and shipbuilding industries. Like other industrial towns along the Cumbrian coast, Barrow-in-Furness is a product of the industrial revolution born of railway mania. The raison d'être for the construction of the railway was that prior to it being conceived 12,000 tons of slate and 60,000 tons of iron ore were being transported annually by horse-drawn carts from mines and quarries to Barrow-in-Furness for export. The inadequacy of horse-drawn transport in the Furness area led to the first mineral railway being conceived in 1843, when engineer James Walker planned to link Kirkby-in-Furness with Barrow with extensions to Dalton, (Lindal) Rampside and Piel Pier.

The Furness Railway Company was promoted by two local aristocratic land-owners, the Duke of Buccleuch, who owned iron ore mines near Dalton-in-Furness and Lindal, and the Earl of Burlington (who later became Duke of Devonshire), who owned slate mines at Kirkby-in-Furness.

Above: Roa Island was once the site of Piel Pier, where minerals were transferred from rail to ship. *Neal Hardy*

Above: The town of Ulverston illustrated here was once linked to the sea by a short canal, whose original purpose was to carry goods and mineral traffic for onward shipment. *Neal Hardy*

Left: Commensurate with the coming of the Furness Railway in 1846, the old Customs & Excise House was built on Roa Island in 1847 to supervise the Walney Channel and port, and remains to this day. *Neal Hardy*

These two principal subscribers were to take a leading role in the founding of the railway. The Furness Railway Act was passed by Parliament and given the Royal Assent on 23 May 1844: 'An Act for making a railway from Rampside and Barrow to Dalton, Lindal and Kirkby Ireleth, in the County Palatine of Lancashire, to be called The Furness Railway.' A clause of the Lords' Committee of 7 May 1844, stated that 'the company should use locomotive engines and that no trains should proceed along the railway within one hundred yards of the road from Dalton to Newton, at a greater speed than six miles per hour.'

The Furness Railway began with two short mineral railways linking the small port at Piel Pier, near Barrow, with Barrow-in-Furness, Kirkby-in-Furness and Dalton-in-Furness. They were built to carry slate from Kirkby and iron from the Dalton quarries to Piel Pier for shipment to Ireland. Both lines were linked at Millwood Junction near Dalton-in-Furness. From Millwood Junction the combined railway ran past the ruins of Furness Abbey to Barrow and served the intermediate station of Rampside. At the latter place the railway crossed a causeway to reach Piel Pier, which was actually situated on Roa Island.

The Furness Railway was opened for mineral traffic on 3 June 1846. The first train to traverse the line ran the following day, carrying slates from Kirkby for shipment to Ireland. On 24 August the line was opened for passenger traffic, although it carried passengers on Sundays only. The service was decidedly primitive, with only one converted sheep truck for passengers.

While the railway was being constructed the company appointed 23-year-old James Ramsden as Locomotive Superintendent in January 1846. Ramsden had a vision for the future of the railway and was later appointed the FR's General Manager, with the company's headquarters based in Barrow-in-Furness. Under his management the company prospered and expanded at the height of the boom of local industries throughout the 1860s. He was appointed the first Mayor of Barrow-in-Furness and became Sir James Ramsden in 1872, to emerge as the foremost figure in the growth of the town and its docks.

Sir Henry Bessemer was also a central character in the industrialisation of Barrow. He invented the most important technique for making steel in the 19th century, by blowing oxygen through pig iron to remove the impurities. The manufacture of steel became easier and quicker, a factor that revolutionised structural engineering. During 1864 James Ramsden formed a company to manufacture steel by the Bessemer process.

Another leading influential figure in Barrow-in-Furness, and co-founder of the line, was the young speculator and industrialist Henry Schneider, who had arrived in Furness in 1839. In 1851 he discovered vast deposits of ore alongside the railway line near Askham and, in partnership with John Hannay, he went on to build blast furnaces in Barrow. Hannay & Co amalgamated with a company founded by Ramsden to form the Barrow Haematite Iron & Steel Company, and the growth of Barrow was under way by the mid-19th century. By the late Victorian era Barrow's Hindpool ironworks with its ten blast furnaces and 18 5-ton Bessemer converters was the largest steelworks in the world, employing more than 5,000 workers. Without the iron and steel works the shipbuilding industry, which was dependent upon steel, would probably not have been established at Barrow in the first place. Schneider's contribution to Barrow-in-Furness is acknowledged with a statue erected in 1891, in Schneider Square, near Barrow Town Hall.

All the foregoing factors set the seal of prosperity for the Furness Railway at the height of the Industrial Revolution. Barrow-in-Furness Strand railway station was the town's first substantial terminus and served the town's four docks. It opened in 1863, having replaced an earlier primitive wooden structure erected in 1846. Barrow Strand station closed in 1882 upon the completion of a new loop line; this included a larger station, named Barrow-in Furness Central. The 'Park Loop' continued north from the Central station to connect with the Dalton to Kirkby-in-Furness direct line at Thwaite Flat Junction near established mines at Park South Junction. Through working was now possible, thus eliminating the need for the reversal of trains from Barrow to Dalton.

To the south the network was extended south from Crooklands (near Dalton) to Ulverston. This was accomplished in two stages, the first from Crooklands to Lindal in May 1851, and the second from Lindal to Ulverston in June 1854. Construction involved complex engineering work, including Lindal Tunnel, which had to be cut through unstable rock. South of

I am indebted to Paul Shackcloth and the Manchester Locomotive Society for these evocative photographs of the Coniston branch. They were taken in the halcyon days of the LMS – just before nationalisation – during the summer of 1947 by Mr Harold D. Bowtell.

The photographs of Coniston station epitomise the rustic essence of a country branch terminus with its own engine shed, signal box and assorted freight wagons. Characteristically, a Fowler 2-6-2 tank engine shunts the goods siding while an 0-6-0 'Cauliflower' is serviced at the engine shed. Meanwhile LYR 'Radial'

2-4-2 tank No 10644 arrives with a local passenger train comprising two coaches. The elevated position of the picturesque Swiss-chalet-style station, in the shadow of Coniston Old Man, affords a fine vista of Coniston Water nestling in the valley below. *Copyright Manchester Locomotive Society*

the tunnel the 4 miles to Ulverston proved to be difficult too, combining two deep cuttings and steep gradients rising to the 78.9-metre summit, which was to be the highest point on the railway, before joining the metals of the Ulverston & Lancaster Railway.

To the north of Barrow-in-Furness the line was extended from Kirkby-in-Furness to Broughton-in-Furness in 1848 to exploit the copper mines. An Act passed on 18 August 1857 formed the Coniston Railway Company, and the extension of the line to Coniston opened on 18 June 1859 for the transport of copper ore and slate from mines to the coast; it was later developed into a line for tourists. Although originally constituted as a separate concern, the Coniston branch was closely associated with the Furness Railway and was absorbed by it in 1862.

The Whitehaven & Furness Junction Railway (incorporated on 21 July 1845)

Work began on the line from Newtown station at Preston Street, Whitehaven, southwards to the port of Ravenglass in 1847, and it was opened in July 1849. It was followed by completion of the line from Ravenglass to Bootle in July 1850,

and lastly Bootle to Broughton-in-Furness, via the evolving industrial town of Millom, in November 1850. Millom and Green Road were known as Holborn Hill and Underhill respectively, and there were halts at Whitbeck and Kirksanton between Bootle and Millom. Fascinatingly, prior to completion of the final segments of the line from Ravenglass and Bootle to Broughton-in-Furness it was necessary for passengers to travel the extra distance by stagecoach.

The ceremonial opening of the finished Whitehaven & Furness Junction Railway, linking Whitehaven with the Furness Railway, took place on 1 November 1850. A special train conveyed the Earl of Lonsdale and his party southbound from Whitehaven to Broughton-in-Furness, where it was joined by a northbound special train with the Earl of Burlington on board.

A contemporary newspaper reported on the ambience of the occasion:

'A pretty triumphal arch had been erected in front of the station and the road thence to the Old King's Head (Broughton) where

'Jubilee' 4-6-0 No 5690 *Leander* slows down for the sharp Foxfield Curve while hauling the up 'Cumbrian Coast Express' on 18 June 1983. *David Hindle*

mine host Tyson rules the roost… A sumptuous dinner was on the table at 1pm with all the culinary tact and skill which have made Mrs Tyson one of the most popular landladies, whilst wines including champagne of equally good quality followed in abundance.'

The completion of this link was evidently a joyous occasion. However, it was not until August 1858 that a Broughton-in-Furness avoiding line, known as the Foxfield Curve, was installed. This obviated the need for trains to and from Whitehaven and Barrow to reverse at Broughton-in-Furness, where there was no turntable. The sharp curve remains to this day, though the line to Broughton-in-Furness and Coniston finally closed to passengers in 1958.

The Ulverston & Lancaster Railway (incorporated on 24 July 1851)

The official opening of the spectacular Ulverston & Lancaster Railway, linking the Furness Railway at Ulverston with Carnforth, took place at Ulverston on 1 September 1857. With the completion of the railway, Grange-over-Sands began to develop into a town and popular seaside resort with grandiose hotels.

Although known as the Ulverston(e) & Lancaster Railway, it did not extend beyond Carnforth Junction. The very difficult coastal route around Morecambe Bay included two cast-iron viaducts spanning the estuaries of the rivers Kent and Leven,

and a substantial walled embankment to prevent encroachment by the sea. Upon opening a special train conveyed guests from Manchester to Ulverston, and on this auspicious occasion the two viaducts were bedecked with ceremonial arches and all the stations along the line were decorated with flowers and bunting.

James Brunlees of Manchester was the engineer for the viaducts and embankments. An experienced engineer, he also designed the longer Solway Viaduct linking England with Scotland. Work on the 500-yard-long Leven Viaduct began on 1 April 1856. It originally incorporated a swing span for shipping serving the then port of Greenodd. Meanwhile further

south at Arnside, the difficulty of the Kent estuary was addressed by the construction of the Arnside or Kent Viaduct, which commenced on 21 October 1856. Construction of both viaducts invoked deep borings through shifting sands, yet despite the considerable difficulties experienced they were completed by August 1857. Henceforth, travellers would no longer be subjected to a hazardous stagecoach service across the treacherous sands of Morecambe Bay. The first decent road in the area was not built until 1820, when the new turnpike was completed between Levens Bridge and Greenodd. However, it was still a long way round Morecambe Bay, so the cross-sands route

Class 8F No 48151 makes an awe-inspiring sight as it crosses the arches of Arnside Viaduct over the Kent estuary on the 30 March 2002. *Peter Fitton*

remained in use right up until the railway took over.

The Furness Railway Company took over the Ulverston & Lancaster Railway and the Coniston Railway in 1862, and the Whitehaven & Furness Junction Railway in 1866. Despite the complexities of massive engineering difficulties, including the construction of six distinctive low viaducts spanning the estuaries of the rivers Kent, Leven, Duddon, Esk, Mite and Irt, the combined railway links led to the birth of the completed coastal railway from Carnforth to Whitehaven in 1857, just 11 years after its initial conception. With direct links to the national railway network,

local people were now less isolated with easier access to the rest of the country. Local industries and commerce were established and the railway was to play a pivotal role in developing West Cumbria's iron, steel and mining industries and shipbuilding at Barrow.

The Furness & Midland Joint Railway

This line was conceived as a joint venture between the Furness and Midland railways, the cost being equally borne by the two companies. The link between Wennington and Carnforth had the advantages of connecting Lancashire

with the West Riding of Yorkshire, while avoiding the complexities of the rail route through Lancaster. It was also a way of linking Yorkshire with Barrow Docks and Scotland via the Cumbrian coastal route. After receiving the Royal Assent in 1863, construction of the joint line began in 1865.

The stations on the line were built to the architectural style of the Furness Railway. The most difficult engineering works encountered were the construction of the 1,124.74-metre (1,230-yard) Melling Tunnel and the viaduct spanning the upper reaches of the River Lune. The line was finally completed in 1867. It preceded the opening of the awesome Settle to Carlisle

BR Standard No 75019 heads a freight on the Furness & Midland Joint line during the twilight of steam in 1968, *David Hindle*

line, which was built by the Midland Railway in 1875 to compete with other companies with a faster and more direct route to Scotland.

Furness Railway branch lines

During 1881 the Isle of Man and Belfast boat trains were transferred from Roe Island's Piel Harbour to Barrow's new Ramsden Dock.

With the opening of the new dock the original Furness Line of 1846 from Barrow to Piel Harbour became a little-used branch line. Consequently the LMS closed it and its two stations at Rampside and Roa Island on 6 July 1936. Also at that time the dock's passenger potential was questionable, with the cessation of the transatlantic service after only six months.

On 26 June 1876 the Furness Railway was connected to the LNWR by a branch line from Arnside to Hincaster Junction (south of Oxenholme). This connecting line was built for the use of mineral trains carrying coke and iron ore from County Durham to the ironworks in and around Barrow-in-Furness. The single track also carried a passenger service between Kendal and Grange, known locally as the 'Kendal Tommy', serving the stations

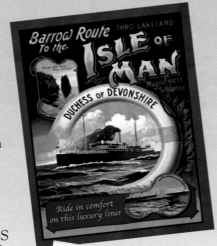

of Sandside and Heversham. The passenger service ended on 4 May 1942, and freight traffic ceased on 9 September 1963. The track between Sandside and Hincaster Junction was lifted in 1966, although a short remnant of track from Arnside to Sandside remained until 31 January 1971, for quarry train workings.

Manufacturing industries led to the construction of branches off the core Furness route to all the major mines, quarries and factories, generating a high volume of freight traffic for the railway. Several mineral lines opened in 1873, including a line to the iron ore mines at Stanton near Roose. In 1874 a mineral line opened from Plumpton Junction near Ulverston to serve the North Lonsdale Iron Works.

The 'Bardsea loop line' was intended as a low-level route to Barrow to avoid the steep gradients at Lindal, but it never got beyond Conishead Priory. The latter station was specially built in the grounds of the priory for the convenience of guests. The Priory became a convalescent home for injured miners in August 1930, and the station was then the terminus of a Durham Miners' train that ran weekly from Co Durham via Barnard Castle, Tebay, Oxenholme and Arnside. Today the only relic of the line

Left: By ferry to the Isle of Man from Ramsden Dock, Barrow. *Bob Gregson railway archive*

Right: A scarce LMS excursion return ticket issued for travel from Heversham to Arnside. *Robert Gregson*

This archaic Class 2F 0-6-0, No 58120, worked the short branches and goods sidings off the Furness line. Note the fireman (extreme right) collecting the token to the former Conishead branch. *Peter Fitton*

Coniston Old Man towers above LYR 'Radial' 2-4-2 tank No 10643 in the beautiful surroundings of Coniston station during August 1947. *Harold D. Bowtell, copyright Manchester Locomotive Society*

from Plumpton Junction to Conishead Priory is the trackbed.

The Furness Railway Company owned several more branch lines, the best-known being the Foxfield to Coniston line and that from Plumpton Junction, south of Ulverston, to Lakeside (Lake Windermere.) These two branch lines eventually became fundamental to the railway's tourism business, with linked sailings on Coniston and Windermere. The Coniston branch opened on 18 June 1859 and was built to serve the copper mines deep in the foothills

of Coniston Old Man. The line climbed from sea level at Foxfield to a summit of 345 feet at Torver, the highest point on the Furness Railway, before entering Coniston station. There were intermediate stations at Broughton-in-Furness, Woodland and Torver.

British Railways closed the Coniston branch to passengers on 4 October 1958 and to goods in 1962. I was saddened by the closure, which was reported in the *North West Evening Mail* on Monday 6 October 1958; I wish I had been a passenger to share

that melancholy occasion. The following is an abridged account of the last diagrammed service on the branch:

'The last passenger service left for Coniston on Saturday 4 October 1958. The 99-year-old "Coniston Flyer" reached the end of the line officially on Saturday to a salvo of railway detonators and a modified chorus of a modern dance tune. A hundred or more passengers made the last sentimental journey through the lovely Lakeland valley – a record send-off for the train that most of them had known all their lives.

The 8.52pm was on time when driver Mr J. A. Watson, of Coniston, whistled her out of the station. On the front of the engine was a notice displaying the words "Foxfield-Coniston, 41217, Oct 4/58, the end". Then it was whistles and waves and an occasional "crack" from a railway detonator all the way up the line. The rain completed the atmosphere. Inside the compartments the passengers spoke of the railwaymen they had known as the train called at Broughton, Woodland and Torver, which by now had seen their last passenger train.

Coniston was the next stop and waiting there to greet the "Flyer" was the station master, Mr J. Lawrence, and a few of the local residents who had braved the weather. Seventy-eight-year-old Mrs M. C. Pearson, of Coniston, stood quietly on the platform to see the last train on a line on which her mother had seen the first. She recalled: "It was only 50 years ago when my husband and I and my nieces and neighbours' children used to walk down to Torver for an outing and then ride back to Coniston for two-and-a-half pennies."

After the "Flyer" had finally pulled into Coniston – five minutes late, but who minded – and the last of the tickets had been autographed by the last of the drivers and firemen, the Class 2 passenger engine

41217 and the rest of the stock steamed back down the line and on to the engine sheds in Barrow. But it was a ghost run that marked the last passenger journey on the nine-and-a-half-mile branch line. Unofficially any of the passengers who had to get back as well were able to make the trip too. The driver, Mr Watson, 19 years on the branch line, starts another job with British Railways at Barrow today, and how does he get there? By bus.'

It was not unusual for an excursion train to run to or from a closed or freight-only station, and thus it was not quite 'the end' for a passenger train to work the Coniston branch. On 27 August 1961 a joint Stephenson Locomotive Society and Manchester Locomotive Society tour of the Furness lines loaded with enthusiasts ran from Manchester. It was hauled along the closed line to Coniston station by 0-6-0 No 44347, then it really was 'the end' for passenger traffic.

The Ulverston to Lakeside branch was constructed to serve the commercial needs of traders at the old port of Greenodd, a gunpowder works at Haverthwaite, and a small ironworks at Backbarrow. The first train ran on 23 April 1869, and passenger trains began calling at the intermediate stations serving the local communities

Another rare example of a ticket issued by the LMS from Bowness Pier, via Lakeside, to the intermediate station of Haverthwaite. *Robert Gregson*

of Greenodd, Haverthwaite and Newby Bridge. It was completed through to Newby Bridge later that year, then extended through to Lakeside a few months later to link with the steamers on Windermere. Lakeside station was formerly a lavish rail/steamer interchange station at the southern tip of Windermere. The Lakeside branch lost its intermediate stations in LMS days; Newby Bridge station closed on 12 September 1939, and Greenodd and Haverthwaite stations on 30 September 1946.

During the early 1960s it became apparent that the era of the rural branch line was about to hit the buffers for good. In accordance with the 'Beeching Report', properly but dubiously named *The Reshaping*

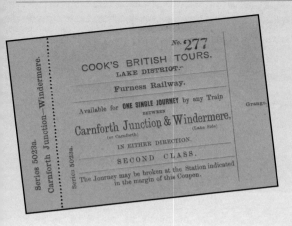

COOK'S BRITISH TOURS.
LAKE DISTRICT.

Furness Railway.

Available for ONE SINGLE JOURNEY by any Train
BETWEEN

Carnforth Junction & Windermere,
(or Carnforth) (Lake Side)

IN EITHER DIRECTION.

SECOND CLASS.

The Journey may be broken at the Station indicated
in the margin of this Coupon.

No. 277

Grange

Series 5023a.
Carnforth Junction—Windermere.
Series 5023a.

An undated Cook's tour of the Lake District. *Bob Gregson railway archive*

of *British Railways*, the Lakeside branch lost its passenger service on 6 September 1965. The steamers were sold by British Railways in the 1980s, although they still operate between Lakeside, Bowness and Ambleside under private ownership.

With the demise of West Cumbria's coal-mining and rich haematite ore industries, the line from Corkickle to Egremont closed on 3 October 1970; likewise the neighbouring line from Egremont to Sellafield closed on 18 January 1980. Only the trackbed remains as evidence of the former mining industry and the local communities the line once served.

The rise and fall of local industries

It was the development of Cumbria's most important burgeoning industries, especially the unearthing of vast amounts of haematite iron ore in the Dalton and Furness areas, that was to be the catalyst for economic growth during the mid-Victorian era.

The area's mineral wealth was to generate huge amounts of traffic for the railway. There were ironworks situated at Carnforth, Ulverston, Askam, Millom and Workington. In 1846 the Carnforth Ironworks Company established a works close to the railway station, which was taken over by the Carnforth Haematite Company in 1864; iron ore was brought in by rail to Carnforth from the Furness area. Coinciding with the coming of the railway to Millom in 1850, the first shafts were sunk at Hodbarrow in the 1850s to reach substantial deposits of iron ore. Consequently by 1881 there were seven pits operated by the Hodbarrow Mining Company. The Millom & Askam Iron Company built Millom Ironworks and the first furnaces were completed in 1866. Like Barrow-in-Furness across the Duddon estuary to the south, the opening of the ironworks led to Millom rising from a hamlet to become Millom Newtown. A second sea wall, the Hodbarrow Outer

Barrier, was completed in 1905 to protect the mines from the sea; it took five years to construct at a cost of almost £600,000.

However, in 1874 manufacturing output was adversely affected by a depression that badly hit the Furness peninsula and parts of Cumberland. This resulted in a reduction of the price of haematite and consequently a crash in the iron and steel industry. Despite peaks and troughs in production, Barrow and the Furness area, including Carnforth Iron Works in Lancashire, were badly hit. Notwithstanding, north-west Cumbria saw the opening of the Derwent iron and steel works at Workington in 1874, and several

Black Combe overlooks the industrial archaeology of Millom, c1970s. The photograph was taken before the pumps were turned off and the mine workings flooded, which gave birth to the large lagoon at the RSPB Hodbarrow Reserve. *David Hindle*

smaller works opened around Workington, albeit to have an ephemeral existence. The 1880s saw further depression in the iron and steel trade with new steel-making processes and imported iron ores. This broke the monopoly of Furness and West Cumberland haematite over the steel trade, and the boom was effectively over by the early 20th century.

Various ore and coal mines in the Workington and Whitehaven area closed between 1910 and the early 1930s and for more than two decades West Cumbria witnessed abject poverty. This was mirrored by soup kitchens and soaring unemployment levels at Workington and Maryport, where the number unemployed reached 86% at the height of the depression. Elsewhere the progressive closure of the industry's ironworks included the closure of Carnforth (1929) and Ulverston (1938). Of the remaining independent works, the huge ironworks at Barrow-in-Furness closed in 1963. Finally the dominant Millom Iron Works crippled employment in the small town when it too closed in 1968, only months after closure of Millom's Hodbarrow iron ore mines.

The discovery of coal in the mid-18th century fast-tracked the growth of Whitehaven until the coal industry collapsed for ever in March 1986 with the closure of Haig Colliery, the last of the town's coal mines. However, by the end of the 19th century the boom years of the local industries were effectively over.

Towards the end of the 19th century industrial contraction gradually climaxed in the erosion of traffic on the main line through West Cumberland. This was a period when the Furness Railway Company was in need of new ideas and new revenue, as we will see in Chapter 3.

Throughout the next two chapters I aim to show how the Furness Railway and the developing railway network changed Wordsworth's beloved Lake District for ever. I examine how excursion traffic to Blackpool became a significant factor in boosting traffic on the Furness Railway and the establishment of Lakeland tourism by the late Victorian era. Wakes Weeks were a legacy of the Industrial Revolution. Many workers simply refused to turn in after only a brief holiday, so mill-owners closed factories to clean and service machines while thousands of their employees enjoyed their annual holiday.

The Cumbrian Coast Line passes through part of the Lake District National Park, which has many literary associations with great names of the past, including Wordsworth, Keats, Coleridge, Ruskin and Beatrix Potter, who were inspired by the local wildlife and landscape. The

2 'The Prelude': Wordsworth's Lakeland

celebrated art and social critic John Ruskin complained that the new railways were unloading trippers like sacks of coal at Windermere.

William Wordsworth was an early conservationist, passionate about protecting the rural beauty of the Lake District, describing it as: 'The loveliest spot that man hath ever found. It is a district of beautiful lakes, of wooded slopes, of waterfalls and glens and of mountains of infinite variety and form.' Wordsworth expressed his doubts about construction of the Furness Railway; on a visit to Furness Abbey on 21 June 1845 he wrote a quite surreal verse about the impending prospect of railway navvies installing the tracks of the railway alongside the abbey:

'We'll have you railway labourers to this ground, withdrawn from labour rest. They sit, they walk among the ruins, but no idle talk is heard; to grave demeanour all are bound; and from one voice a hymn with tuneful sound hallows once more the long deserted quire and thrills the old sepulchral earth, around. Others look up, and with fixed eyes admire that all spanned arch, wondering how it was raised, to keep so high in the air, its strength and grace: all seem to feel the spirit of the place, and by the general reference God is praised: Profane despoilers, stand yet not reproved, while thus these simple-hearted men are moved.'

Wordsworth's doggerel verse was to no avail and work on installing the railway went relentlessly ahead, and the first passenger service on the Furness Railway ran on 24 August 1846.

In 1844 the proposed Kendal and Windermere railway line threatened to encroach upon his treasured Lake District and he responded with a literary campaign. In a letter to the *Morning Post* published on 16 October 1844 he wrote that there was no need for a railway in close proximity to the Lake District: 'There were no manufacturers, quarries or a substantial agriculture base to warrant the intrusion.' In a letter to the Prime Minister, William Gladstone, on 15 October 1844 he backed up his plea by enclosing a poem that began, 'Is there no nook of English ground secure from rash assault?' Despite Wordworth's interventions, the Kendal to Windermere line opened on 22 April 1847. It is perhaps an irony that for many years the Furness Railway and Lakeland branch lines have provided a sustainable alternative to disproportionate car traffic on the area's narrow roads.

Railway mania: the birth of a railway revolution

With the coming of the Furness Railway and five branch lines, including the narrow-gauge Ravenglass & Eskdale Railway, which opened in 1876, social and leisure groups all began to use the railway network to discover Lakeland for pleasure. There was so much to see and do on the branch lines to Lakeside and Coniston, though doubtless neither William Wordsworth nor John Ruskin would have approved of such an intrusion!

The Lancaster & Carlisle Railway extended its line over Shap to reach Carlisle in 1846, and Glasgow in 1848. Thereafter the route was taken over by the London & North Western Railway in

An 0-6-0 'Cauliflower'-hauled passenger train arrives at Keswick station. *Robert Gregson railway archive*

A contemporary postcard of Keswick and Derwentwater. Note Keswick station in the foreground and its covered walkway to the adjacent Keswick Railway Station Hotel. *Robert Gregson railway archive*

1866 and formed part of the main Anglo-Scottish main line (the West Coast Main Line), giving more rail access to the lakes on the eastern fringe. The Cockermouth, Keswick & Penrith (CK&P) line officially opened for passenger traffic on 2 January 1865, with trains running to and from a new joint station at Cockermouth, close to Wordsworth's birthplace.

To the dismay of Wordsworth, the public began to discover Lakeland following the era of railway mania, a term describing the utter frenzy of railway construction in the Victorian era. Railway mania was no less applicable to the Furness Railway and its integrated lines in 1845/46 at the time of Wordsworth's visit to Furness

Abbey. Although the Furness Railway Act was given the Royal Assent on 23 May 1844, railway mania actually reached its zenith in 1846, when no fewer than 272 Acts of Parliament were passed to set up new railway companies. Nationally, the proposed routes totalled 9,500 miles (15,300km) of new railway.

Further afield, railway mania was to impact on the Furness Railway, especially during Wakes Weeks. On 15 July 1840 the Preston & Wyre Railway was opened, connecting Preston with Fleetwood, with ambitious plans for the development of the latter place as a port – Fleetwood was

created by the railway. It was not until February 1846 that a branch from the Preston & Wyre line at Poulton-le-Fylde to Blackpool (North) established Blackpool as a popular seaside resort.

The construction of the Furness Railway and the new extensive railway network meant that the seaside resorts along the north-west coast of Lancashire, Westmorland and Cumberland came within easy reach of industrial Lancashire during the time of the wakes. Blackpool developed into a flourishing seaside resort in the late 19th century with a catchment

Thousands of people arrived at Blackpool during the wakes. The significance of the resort's railway excursions is relevant to the development of the Furness Railway. *Bob Gregson railway archive*

area embracing the mill towns of Lancashire and Yorkshire and other great centres of industry. The popularity of Blackpool was demonstrated during the 1919 Nelson Wakes when 10,000 people from the small town of Nelson lodged at the resort for a minimum of four days.

Numerous excursions were packed with excited families, who flocked to Blackpool to catch an early glimpse of the newly constructed Blackpool Tower and the neighbouring 'Big Wheel'. Many of Blackpool's famous attractions were built in the latter half of the 19th century, including North Pier (1863), Central Pier (1868), South Pier (1894), and the world-famous Blackpool Tower (1894). More than 23,000 holidaymakers travelled on special trains from Oldham alone to the resort during 1860.

The traditional Wakes Weeks spread throughout Lancashire and the season was prolonged at Blackpool from mid-July to mid-September. With an established railway network by 1870, the number of excursions increased dramatically with crowds of people travelling to Lancashire's seaside resorts, some of whom enjoyed combined steamer cruises to the Lake District.

Paddle steamers sailing from Blackpool's North Pier. *Bob Gregson railway archive*

By paddle steamer to the Furness peninsula

By 1865 Wordsworth's Lakeland could be reached by the national and local railway network via the Furness Railway and all the Lakeland branch lines. Significantly, Lakeland could also be reached by the numerous paddle steamers sailing from Blackpool, Fleetwood and Morecambe. In my 19th-century 'Bradshaw's Guide' first published in 1863 there is a reference to Blackpool, which is linked with the development of Victorian tourism to the Lake District. It describes Blackpool as

'...a pretty bathing place situated on a range of cliffs fronting the Irish Sea ... fine views of the Cumberland and Welsh hills and the Isle of Man can be obtained from several spots about here. In 1863, a new pier was opened which forms a pleasant promenade. During the season great facilities are offered for excursions to Furness Abbey, Ulverston and Coniston.'

As early as 1840 (before the opening of the Furness Railway in August 1846), passengers made the crossing of Morecambe Bay by paddle steamer operating from Fleetwood to Bardsea, near Ulverston. On 18 July of that year the steamer service was advertised by the *Preston Pilot* thus:

'The shortest and best way to the lakes is by the fine steamer, *The Express*, which contains first class accommodation for passengers, carriages and horses. This will afford the quickest, cheapest and most agreeable route to the lakes and other attractions of that most agreeable district.'

Thus the potential of 'that most agreeable district' had been realised. Passengers were now able to discover the hills and mountains of the Lake District by carriage, while taking in fresh, clean air, far away from the grime and pollution of the Industrial Revolution.

Following the opening of the Furness Railway to Piel Pier on Roa Island in June 1846, a combined boat and rail passenger service was inaugurated in August. The steamer between Fleetwood and Piel Pier carried no fewer than 1,500 passengers a week, of whom more than 500 were visitors to the ruins of Furness Abbey. The Furness Railway Company took care of the ruins on behalf of the Cavendish family, and even appointed a guide to show visitors round.

The Earl of Burlington despairingly commenting that 'after the train returns to Piel the mob vanishes.' Despite his patronising comments, tourism was encouraged. The Furness Railway Company purchased the old Manor House in 1847, and converted it to the aptly named Furness Abbey Hotel. During London's Great Exhibition of 1851, railway passengers were carried to Piel for the steamer to Morecambe; this was prior to the completion of the Ulverston & Lancaster Railway in 1857, hence the necessary boat crossing of Morecambe Bay. With excursions converging at the London exhibition site from all parts of the country, travel mobility was under way for masses of people, and travel by rail had opened up England. Poignantly, rail travel was also beginning to open up Wordsworth's Lakeland to tourism.

The late 19th century brought an increase in leisure time, which few but the rich had been able to enjoy before; the five-and-a-half-day working week had become increasingly accepted from the 1860s. The 1871 Bank Holiday Act extended the number of public holidays to cover Easter Monday, Whit Monday, Boxing Day and August Bank Holiday, in addition to Christmas Day and Good Friday. By the 1890s most workers enjoyed at least one week's holiday a year, while at the same time many people had more money to spend on leisure. Holidaymakers visited the Lancashire coast and the Lake District as well as a handful of small Victorian and Edwardian resorts dotted along the Cumbrian coast; Silverdale, Arnside, Grange-over-Sands and Seascale in particular became quite popular holiday resorts along the route of the Furness Railway.

Piel Pier continued to be used until the various steamer services moved to a new steamer berth near the entrance to Ramsden Dock in 1882. The old pier was removed in 1891 after falling into a state of disrepair. However, a major tourist link from Fleetwood to Ramsden Dock was to be established from 1895.

3 'Hindle Wakes' to the growth of leisure and tourism

During the late Victorian era the decline of local industries began to impact on the Furness Railway's freight traffic to such an extent that the focus switched to the development of tourism. During the company's glory year, this was achieved by the implementation of combined tours of the Lake District by excursion train, coach and steam boat. At the turn of the 20th century, under the leadership of its new General Manager, Alfred Aslett, the Furness Railway was transformed from a run-down industrial line into a tourist line.

The enjoyment of the Furness Railway by the Victorians and Edwardians

The era of mass tourism to the Lake District really got under way from 1895 with combined steamer and rail cruises departing from Fleetwood Port to Barrow's Ramsden Dock. It was pioneered by Alfred Aslett, who was appointed Secretary of the Furness Railway in 1895 and General Manager in 1896, following the death of the previous incumbent, Sir James Ramsden. The new manager had previously worked in a similar capacity on the Cambrian Railways and doubtless proved to be the right man for the job.

Alfred Aslett was appointed General Manager of the Furness Railway in 1896 and quickly established Lakeland tourism. *Bob Gregson railway archive*

The Furness Railway Company set about improving services and facilities. Aslett pioneered cheap weekly fares, with tickets allowing up to six journeys a week between any two stations, and cheap day tickets to popular resorts and other concessions for short breaks. It was claimed that the Furness stations were without equal for cleanliness and convenience. It was really a matter of

refocusing the business and putting Furness and the Lake District firmly on the national map. New services were introduced from Euston, Manchester, Leeds and Cambridge, as well as the Belfast boat trains at Heysham Port. To popularise the Isle of Man route via Barrow, Aslett negotiated with the North Eastern Railway for a through summer service from Newcastle-upon-Tyne, operating from 1 July 1905.

A description of an Edwardian railway tour of Cumbria to attract increasing numbers of day trippers to the Lake District by rail was promoted by the company. This comprised promotional posters designed to attract visitors, with smaller versions issued as a set of postcards in a special envelope, sold for threepence.

Aslett was quick to realise that the railway was fundamental to the future of tourism in the Lake District. The company increased the number of combined rail and coach tours from only four to 20 throughout the summer months. Large coloured posters of Lakeland and coastal resorts were displayed at railway stations and elsewhere to attract holidaymakers. At Blackpool a handcart was laden with posters

Above: A Furness Railway poster depicted the fastest route to Lakeland by steamer from Fleetwood. *Bob Gregson railway archive*

Attractive English Lakeland posters issued by the Furness Railway Company were displayed at railway stations. Note that several advertise Alfred Aslett's combined tours, at the time when he was Secretary and General Manager. *Bob Gregson railway archive*

withdrawn in 1870, as a means of attracting holidaymakers from Blackpool to visit the Lake District. The tour commenced at Blackpool and, on arrival at Fleetwood, passengers embarked on the paddle steamer PS *Lady Evelyn*, introduced in 1900, for the 1½-hour cruise to Ramsden Dock, Barrow. Departing from Fleetwood at 10.15am, passengers paid 3 shillings for the return journey, with tourist tickets available for an unlimited number of crossings over seven days from May to the end of September.

Between 1900 and 1910 this vessel was joined by four additional paddle steamers operating the same route: PS *Lady Margaret* (1903), PS *Lady Philomena* (1908), PS *Philomel* (1908), and finally PS *Lady Moyra* (1910). During the bay crossing refreshments and entertainment were provided as well as an opportunity to be photographed by Barrow photographer Edward Sankey. Poignantly, the good ship *Lady Evelyn* ended her days at the evacuation of Dunkirk in 1940.

The company claimed a

'...great success attendant upon the Company's enterprise in opening out the service from Blackpool to the Lakes, via Fleetwood and Barrow. It has been due to the excellent arrangements made and the conveniences provided. The popularity

promoting the Aslett tours of the Lake District. The concept was to beguile holidaymakers visiting Blackpool to also visit the Lake District by offering an integrated rail and road Lake District sightseeing tour with a combined sea crossing of Morecambe Bay from Fleetwood to Barrow-in-Furness.

In 1901 Aslett reinstated a two-way Fleetwood to Barrow steamer crossing of Morecambe Bay, which had been

An LYR/LNWR railway information pavilion on Blackpool promenade advertised tours to the Lakes and Fleetwood. *Bob Gregson railway archive*

Fleetwood station in Victorian times. The steamer crossing of the bay to link up with Furness Railway excursions began here. *Bob Gregson railway archive*

Aslett's tours enabled the public to discover the beauty of Thirlmere, overshadowed by the formidable Helvellyn. *Bob Gregson railway archive*

of this service has been greatly enhanced since the acquisition of the PS *Lady Moyra*, carrying 1,013 passengers, with a speed of 19 knots. This steamer in conjunction with the PS *Lady Evelyn* is admirably adapted for the development of the Furness Company's tourist traffic between the populous centres of Lancashire and the Lake District.'

By 1906 a combined rail, sea, lake and coach tour was advertised by coloured posters and in the annual special guide book as 'The Outer Circular'. The tour cost 7s 6d at a time when a good wage was £1 a week, thus amounting to nearly a third of that wage. On arrival at Ramsden Dock station, trippers boarded the train for Lakeside to join the steamer sailing the full length of Windermere to Ambleside. From Ambleside passengers were transported to Coniston station for the return train journey via Foxfield to Barrow and the bay crossing to Fleetwood. The success of this combined tour led to an increase in the number of passengers patronising the Fleetwood to Barrow steamer route to 127,000 by 1910.

Around 1912 motor charabancs superseded carriages on circular tours, and Aslett took great pride in his 'Six Lakes Tour', incorporating Windermere, Ullswater, Derwentwater, Thirlmere, Grasmere and Rydal Water.

Taking to the roads in an open-top charabanc with oilskins, rugs and umbrellas was in those days an adventure for the intrepid passengers. The tour cost 13 shillings and included steamer fares on Windermere and Ullswater and coach and rail travel. Another shorter tour cost 4s 3d and visited the medieval Cartmel

Fortuitously, the elegant SY *Gondola* still plies up and down the lake in time-honoured fashion to this day. *Peter Fitton*

MV *Tern* sails the tranquil waters of Windermere on 9 September 2001. *Peter Fitton*

Bygone Windermere steamers are berthed at Lakeside Pier adjacent to the impressive Furness Railway station and cafeteria. *Robert Gregson*

Priory and the home of the Cavendish family at Holker Hall. The company promoted the ruins of Furness Abbey and the Furness Abbey Hotel, a luxuriously appointed facility owned by the company, which boasted 36 bedrooms. (It is now demolished.)

The Furness Railway Company operated steamers on both Windermere and Coniston Water. The first steamer service on an English lake was inaugurated on Windermere in the summer of 1845 with the SS *Lady of the Lake*. The FR took over the Windermere Steam Yacht Company in 1872 and operated services on both Windermere and Coniston Water. Subsequent publicity claimed that

'...the fleet of steam yachts on Windermere are the best of their kind, and a trip on the lake, or an extended tour through Lakeland is immensely enhanced by a journey in these delightful steamers.'

On the Coniston branch line a quaint steam carriage was introduced in 1905. On Coniston Water the company's steam yacht *Gondola*, built in 1859, continued operating until 1939; it then fell into a state of dereliction from which it was rescued and restored to service by the National Trust in 1980.

At the beginning of the 20th century Wordsworth's Lakeland had become a haven for tourists, and in 1910 alone a staggering three million-plus passengers travelled on the Furness Railway. Unfortunately, there were dark clouds on the horizon, and the First World War was looming. The key boat crossing from Fleetwood to Barrow-in-Furness finished with the outbreak of war in 1914, and the ships were disposed of. The Barrow to Belfast boat train and the Isle of Man and connecting boat trains also ceased to operate from that year.

Alfred Aslett retired from his post as Manager in 1918 at the age of 71. Despite economic gloom and depression, the outbreak of the First World War and the advent of motor cars, he nevertheless left behind a railway in good shape. Today, some of Aslett's tours can be followed by bus, lake and rail, including the steam-operated Lakeside & Haverthwaite heritage line. Sadly, with the closure of branch lines and bus routes, certain tours now have to be undertaken by car.

Victorian seaside resorts served by the Furness Railway and social change

Despite expectations seaside villages and small towns along the Cumbrian coast were not transformed into thriving seaside resorts and never attracted masses of people, although the Furness Railway Company attempted to popularise several genteel resorts served by the railway. To a modest degree it succeeded, but neither Arnside nor Grange-over-Sands became the resorts envisaged, despite Edwardian Grange being dubbed 'The Torquay of the North'. Pleasure boats sailed from the stone jetty at Arnside and steamboats came across the bay from both Blackpool and Morecambe to Grange, but were restricted by the tides. There were also trips to Holme Island from Grange.

Further north on the Cumberland coast, Seascale failed to develop as a bustling resort, once hailed as the 'Bournemouth of

the North' – subject to the vagaries of the imagination, I think! This was despite Sir James Ramsden promoting an ambitious plan to develop it in 1879. The Scawfell Hotel was built adjacent to the railway station and Seascale was promoted as a holiday resort. Victorian advertising made much of the fine beach, and as a base for exploring the western Lake District. However, the hotel was no panacea for the impulsive days of Victorian optimism, and it failed. This last remnant of Ramsden's hopes for Seascale was demolished in 1997, but if the crowds envisaged had come to enjoy the resort we might have had another Blackpool!

Silecroft, too, has fine beaches and witnessed moderate numbers of seasonal holidaymakers and day trippers in the early 20th century, but has remained as a quiet undersized resort. At Millom it was events on the industrial front that forestalled any potential for tourism. In 1850 it was only a small settlement centred on Holborn Hill, where there was a railway halt bearing the name Holborn. Coinciding with the exploitation of the biggest deposit of haematite iron ore in the world, which was discovered in 1856, the hamlet began to expand into a small industrial town with a brand-new station named Millom.

Despite the success during the Alfred

Seascale beach as seen from the railway station in the early 20th century. The Victorian resort failed to develop as the 'Bournemouth of the North'. *Robert Gregson*

Aslett era, the commercialisation of leisure depended on the amount and proportion of working-class incomes that could be spared. The reality is that the wealthy Victorian middle-class tourists and holidaymakers had defined tastes while visiting venues such as Furness Abbey, Grange-over-Sands or Seascale. Unlike the more wealthy Victorian tourists to the area, the working classes were more content to rely on local attractions. Train services were not excessively patronised by the local working classes, who perhaps by necessity preferred to stay at home because they couldn't afford the fares.

4 A journey along the Furness Railway – the line that time forgot

'The train now standing at Platform 5 is for all stations to Whitehaven. Today's excursion will call at Carnforth, Silverdale, Arnside, Grange-over-Sands, Kent's Bank, Cark and Cartmel, Ulverston (for Lakeside), Dalton, Roose, Barrow, Askham, Kirkby-in-Furness, Foxfield (for Coniston), Green Road, Millom, Silecroft, Bootle, Ravenglass, Drigg, Seascale, Sellafield, Braystones, Nethertown, St Bees, Corkickle and Whitehaven Bransty.'

In this chapter I describe a journey north from Carnforth to Whitehaven with various features to observe along the line and stop-offs at many of the quaint and numerous stations that are so characteristic of the Cumbrian Coast Line.

The railway scene of yesteryear in Furness came complete with freight sidings, coal yards, gas and oil lamps, timber crossings, quaint signal boxes, semaphore signals, cheery station staff, wooden platforms, and stations with a distinctive Furness Railway style of red brick architecture. Paradoxically many of these features, including the original Furness stations and halts, crossings and signal boxes, survive to this day to remind passengers of the line's illustrious past.

It is a long meandering railway line from Carnforth to Whitehaven, with around 24 'back of beyond' wayside stations and halts that barely any person has ever heard of. Remarkably most of them outlived the Beeching 'axe', to sustain the needs of local residents, commuters, day trippers and tourists. What is, perhaps, not generally known is that several stations were originally designed by the renowned architects Austin & Paley of Lancaster; these include Silverdale, Grange-over-Sands, Ulverston, Askam, Foxfield, Bootle and Whitehaven. Despite the demise of the mineral and other principal industries served by the Furness Railway, the core route survives.

With the sea and the shores of Morecambe Bay on one side, and a scenic landscape interspersed with dramatic views of the Lake District on the other, it is well worth taking a day out just for unfettered pleasure. However, before commencing the journey I recommend a visit to the station café and heritage centre at Carnforth, where you will be pleasantly surprised, especially if you are a film buff.

Brief Encounter

We begin our journey at Carnforth railway station, whose refreshment room provided the model for the set of the classic black and white 1945 film *Brief Encounter*. This

Celia Johnson and Trevor Howard on set for the film *Brief Encounter*. *Bob Dobson railway archive*

was perhaps director David Lean's most famous and romantic British film, telling of a love affair between Laura Jesson (Celia Johnson) and Dr Alex Harvey (Trevor Howard)

The film begins with a commentary by Laura Jesson: 'It all started on an ordinary day, in the most ordinary place in the world – the refreshment room at Milford Junction … That's how it all began, through me getting a little piece of grit in my eye [common in the days of steam trains]. I completely forgot the whole incident; at least I thought I had. But then next Thursday I met him again.'

This atmospheric picture was filmed on location at Carnforth against a setting of LMS steam locomotives and trains such as the prestigious 'Coronation Scot' and 'Royal Scot', steaming through the station. Interestingly, it was supposed to be Milford Junction, notwithstanding that the romantic couple walked past a semaphore direction indicator clearly stating Hellifield, Skipton, Leeds and Bradford, a complete give-away for Carnforth station!

The renowned station café typically served mugs of tea, cheese on toast and all the usual fare. The great Stanley Holloway, dressed in LMS uniform, complemented the scene while chatting with the woman behind the counter. In the background there was a station announcement made by Noel Coward. Here, to the accompaniment of Sergei Rachmaninov's 2nd Piano Concerto, a brief encounter progressed favourably after the gentlemanly Dr Harvey removed that confounded piece of grit from the lady passenger Laura's eye. Dr Harvey took his newly found ladyfriend to the local cinema, and so began a romance – outwardly innocent? Perhaps not, for

Above: The original famous station clock is still in situ at the top of Carnforth station's subway. *David Eaves*

Right: Majestic trains like the prestigious 'Coronation Scot' once roared through Carnforth station. *Bob Gregson railway archive*

one is left to believe that their newly found relationship was approaching infidelity, but surely not, for those were more discreet times!

When the station clock calls time on their amorous flirtations, it is time to ascend the famed subway and meet for a final brief encounter. Woefully, this tender moment is impolitely interrupted by Laura's friend at an inopportune time, at which point Dr Harvey suddenly boards a train bound for South Africa. Thereafter Laura abstains from meeting a passing express head on and banishes thoughts of suicide. She returns home to her husband, although apparently in a lovesick trance. A seemingly ambivalent husband gently informs her that 'whatever your dream was it was not a very happy one.' The plot and the wonderful music have by now reached their climax and hopefully all parties involved lived happily ever after – or did they?

What is not in dispute is that today the fully restored clock manufactured in the 19th century by Joyce of Whitworth, and featured in a timeless moment in the film, still ticks away at the top of the subway on Platform 1. The 1930s café has carefully been restored to resemble the film set and is waiting to transport the customer back in time to experience their own brief encounter; meanwhile the film is shown on

a loop in the replica room.

To recreate the complete scenario, why not reflect in comfort in the legendary refreshment room with a cup of tea and witness the power of a preserved steam locomotive thundering through Carnforth just like it did in the film? Tourists come from all over the world to visit the romantic film location and heritage centre to see where it all started. It is certainly well worth a visit and the crowning moment might be to experience your own 'brief encounter' – who knows?

It was in 1846 that the first railway station was opened at Carnforth as a simple wayside halt, but by 1880 it had emerged as a major railway junction of three railways. The Furness ran its service to Barrow and Whitehaven, the London & North Western Railway operated the main line, and the Furness & Midland Joint line came in from Wennington. Carnforth was always the most southerly point of the Furness line.

With the coming of the railway Carnforth started to grow from a small village into a railway town. The growth was accentuated by the Carnforth Haematite Iron Company's works, which were capable of producing 3,000 tons of pig iron per week. The huge Victorian furnaces that were once used for smelting the pig iron for Bessemer steel would have been visible from

Class 37 No 37409 leaves Carnforth with the morning service from Preston to Barrow on 10 September 2015. Note the 1882 Furness Railway signal box at the end of the platform. *Mark Bartlett*

The same train passes under the old Carnforth Iron Works tram road bridge. *Mark Bartlett*

the train north-west of Carnforth station.

The quirky disued 1882 signal box at the north end of Carnforth station formerly adjoined the station's all-encompassing roof. Close examination of the Grade II-listed signal box reveals the Furness Railway coat of arms below the gable. Furness signal boxes were usually of a pleasing architectural design and that at Carnforth is no exception. The station itself is architecturally interesting. When reconstructed in 1937 it boasted the longest unsupported single-piece concrete roof in Britain.

Leaving Carnforth, on the left-hand side we see rows of the West Coast Railway's diesel locomotives and rolling stock. They are based at the former British Railways Motive Power Depot and used on heritage trains throughout the country. Close by, the soaring concrete coaling tower stands like a sentinel in commemoration to the Steam Age. Indeed, it is the last surviving giant coaling tower in the country. The steam depot opened in 1944, built for the London Midland & Scottish Railway, and closed in 1968.

A little further along the line the first views of Morecambe Bay and its wildlife emerge. The windswept

marshes and tidal creeks are, in my opinion, symbolic of the remote beauty and grandeur of the bay.

Nowadays Silverdale station is dubbed 'Silverdale – the home of Leighton Moss', although the scattered coastal village is situated about a mile from the station. Leighton Moss is one of the North West's best year-round birdwatching sites, supporting an excellent range of reed-bed, wetland and woodland birds. The moss is set in glorious scenery, provided by the backdrop of limestone woodland, heath and rolling farmland. Wildlife is viewable from superb hides and there are plenty of

facilities, including a café and visitor centre. The RSPB reserve is famous for its otters, red deer and rare bird species, including bittern, bearded tit, marsh harrier and much more. The reserve is well worthy of exploration (see Walk 1, Chapter 13).

Silverdale is a good place to disembark from the train, which is something I started doing in 1957 with three or four friends, usually on a Sunday. The steam trains must have been long in those days, because the carriages regularly exceeded the length of Silverdale's station platform. We found ourselves way off the platform on arrival, and ended up at the next station, Arnside.

Class 153 Nos 153332 and 153330 call at Silverdale station, now dubbed 'Silverdale – the home of Leighton Moss', forming a Barrow to Lancaster service on 6 June 2016. *Mark Bartlett*

The shy and elusive bittern is famous for its vocal 'booming' and is one of the highlights of Silverdale's Leighton Moss Reserve. *Peter Smith*

By necessity we discovered a coastal walk via White Creek and Far Arnside to Silverdale (Walk 2). There are numerous walks to be discovered from both Silverdale and Arnside stations around the Silverdale and Arnside Area of Outstanding Natural Beauty.

After leaving Silverdale station the line passes the prominent grey and roofless ruin of Arnside Tower, which still graces the landscape as a forlorn sentinel to the invader. It is a late-medieval tower house (or peel tower) and was originally five storeys high. Tower houses were often built in the insecure areas of northern England and the Scottish border and were intended as watch towers where signal fires could be lit by the garrison to warn of approaching danger. The limestone tower suffered a serious fire in 1602 but, after repairs, it remained in use until the end of the 17th century; the designated Ancient Monument is now in a ruinous state.

The small coastal settlement of Arnside is thought to take its name from a Viking called Arnulf when it became his family *saetr* or seat. Before the coming of the railway Arnside, Sandside and Milnthorpe flourished as small estuarine ports. The

railway first came to Arnside in 1857 and established the Victorian resort with its characteristic Victorian shops and houses. The town is dominated by Arnside Knott, standing 522 feet above sea level; its summit is easily walkable from the station and from it the magnificent view of the wide sweep of Morecambe Bay and the Lakeland mountains makes a visit well worthwhile (Walk 2).

Arnside station was once the junction for the Furness branch line serving

Sandside and Heversham. The trackbed can still be seen veering off in a north-easterly direction towards the West Coast Main Line, which it joined at Hincaster Junction.

Arnside is the starting point for the cross-bay walks to Kent's Bank and the Westmorland Way walk through gorgeous limestone countryside. A siren warns of the incoming tide and the 'Kent bore', which is decidedly not a grumpy old man of the resort, but a local tidal spectacle.

The panoramic view of Morecambe Bay from Arnside Knott features Ivatt 2-6-0 No 46441 crossing Arnside Viaduct on 21 August 1964. *Peter Fitton*

The initial tidal surge varies in strength and speed, and very quickly it submerges the bay's intertidal sand flats.

After leaving Arnside the train makes the crossing of the River Kent over the first of five distinctive low estuarial viaducts that feature so prominently along the line. Having crossed the 457-metre-long structure the line runs close to the shore along a long stone embankment dotted with rare and delicate fronds of maidenhair fern. On the seaward side is a causeway linking the shore with the privately owned Holme Island. This was once the home of John Brogden, an industrialist who was the promoter and builder of the Ulverston & Lancaster Railway. Inland the limestone rocks of Whitbarrow Scar are impressive.

The next station, Grange-over-Sands, is a classic Austin & Paley creation built between 1864 and 1872, and is a Grade II-listed building. With the arrival of the railway

Above: The Kent Viaduct underwent major structural improvements for a period of 16 weeks between March and July 2011. Throughout that period trains terminated at Arnside, seen here on 7 April. *Mark Bartlett*

Right: Class 37 No 37402 propels the Saturdays-only Carlisle to Lancaster service over the Kent Viaduct on 15 October 2016. *Mark Bartlett*

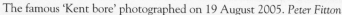

The famous 'Kent bore' photographed on 19 August 2005. *Peter Fitton*

Class 5 4-6-0 No 44932 crosses over the River Winster at its confluence with Morecambe Bay on the approach to Grange. *David Eaves*

in 1857 Grange developed from a small fishing village to a popular but small resort. Wealthy factory-owners from Lancashire and Yorkshire could now reach Grange in a couple of hours, so began to build more holiday houses.

The 'over-Sands' suffix was added in the late Victorian era by the local clergy, who became tired of their mail going to the other Grange-in-Borrowdale in the Lake District. The suffix today is a contradiction, as they are mudflats with dangerous quicksands that have increasingly developed into a dense meadow of spartina, a plant that has colonised large areas of the sand flats of the bay, including intertidal areas of Grange-over-Sands. Today many day trippers just like to stroll along the promenade to the site of the old open-air baths and back, observing some of the birds of the bay (Walk 3).

A short distance from Grange may be found the limestone outcrop known as Hampsfell. The summit is worth the ascent for it affords extensive views of Morecambe Bay.

Kent's Bank, a suburb of Grange, has its own station, which is now unstaffed. This station serves thousands of walkers who cross the sands and tidal creeks of

Stanier 2-6-4T No 42594 arrives at Grange with the morning Barrow to Morecambe train on 29 July 1963. *Peter Fitton*

Ivatt 2-6-0 No 46426 arrives at Grange station with a Morecambe to Lakeside train on the same day. *Peter Fitton*

Morecambe Bay from Arnside, or Hest Bank, while under the safe supervision of the Queen's Guide.

Within easy reach of Kent's Bank station is another limestone knoll, known as Humphrey Head, which can be seen from the train bulging into the bay like a huge leviathan having a nap. Humphrey Head comprises a nature reserve of the Cumbria Wildlife Trust, which supports a rare limestone flora featuring the exceedingly rare goldilocks and several species of rare ferns. It is claimed that the last wild wolf

in England was killed here by huntsmen in 1390. Fact or fable – who knows?

Thereafter the line leaves the coast for a while and veers inland through appealing pastoral countryside to arrive at the next station, Cark & Cartmel, serving both the villages in the name. It is the station for Cartmel Races and the medieval Cartmel Priory and Holker Hall, the home of the Cavendish family. Cartmel is one of the most interesting villages in the district, with a charming market square complementing the medieval priory. The venerable church

is Grade I-listed and has long been of considerable interest to both tourists and discerning historians. It is of the Norman and early English architectural style, and the walls of the chancel are said to be the oldest part of the building. In the burial records for Cartmel Priory are many who perished while crossing the notorious sands of Morecambe Bay, long before the coming of the railway.

Holker Hall is fascinating and well worth a visit. It is situated on the east bank of the Leven estuary amidst tastefully laid-

Class 37 No 37425 accelerates away from Grange station, alongside the promenade, with a Preston to Barrow train on 28 December 2016. *Mark Bartlett*

Class 'V2' No 4771 *Green Arrow* crosses the Leven Viaduct on 21 September 1974. *Peter Fitton*

out gardens and an extensive woodland estate that slopes down to the edge of the River Leven.

Shortly after leaving Cark & Cartmel station the Furness line passes along a long stone embankment leading onto the 457.2-metre-long Leven Viaduct, the line's second major such structure. It spans the River Leven and provides opportunities to see from the carriage window flocks of wigeon, mallard, teal, shelduck, eider, redshank, oystercatcher, curlew, heron and the now abundant little egret.

Beyond the wildfowl and waders the remote and uninhabited Chapel Island may be seen way out in the estuary. The island has been known to lure curious tourists, but dangerous channels and quicksand should be avoided at all costs! Chapel Island got its present name in 1795, because of its association with Conishead Priory. In the 14th century Cistercian monks from the priory built a small chapel on the island

For me, crossing the viaducts on the Cumbrian Coast Line has always been an exciting and breathtaking experience with so much to see, including this drake eider duck. *Geoff Carefoot*

of 28 February 1903 a particularly violent storm broke out over the North West coast. This resulted in the down Barrow mail train being brought to an emergency stop near the centre of the viaduct, but a fierce gust of wind blew several carriages onto their sides. Fortunately they did not fall over the low parapet into the water below, and there was no loss of life, but 33 people were injured. The engine and a mail sorting van remained on the rails and the line was cleared for normal traffic within 9 hours.

On leaving the viaduct the course of the Lakeside branch may be observed veering off to the right. At Plumpton Junction a short branch once led west to the North Lonsdale Iron Works and Conishead Priory. The single line latterly served the pharmaceutical plant of Glaxo Smith Kline as well as Conishead Priory, but the track has now been lifted.

Approaching Ulverston the main line crosses the Ulverston Canal, which was built for the shipment of iron ore from

to serve the needs of fishermen working in the Leven fisheries. Nothing remains of the chapel, although ruins were still extant in 1774. There was also a cottage on the island, probably built in the early 19th century, which was ostensibly occupied by fishermen.

The Leven Viaduct was once the scene of a serious accident, which could have had dire consequences bearing similarities to the Tay Bridge disaster. In the early hours

Class 5 4-6-0 No 44982 passes Plumpton Junction with the last Blackpool to Lakeside service train on 3 September 1965. Also featured is the former branch to Conishead Priory veering off to the right. *Peter Fitton*

Class 37 No 37418 *Pectinidae* passes Plumpton Junction on 25 April 1992 with the 12.08 Barrow to Lancaster train. *Peter Fitton*

Lindal, and it remains as a legacy of the industrialisation of the Furness landscape to this day. To the right is Hoad Hill with its monument erected in 1850 to the memory of Sir John Barrow, one of Ulverston's worthy sons. The Grade II-listed monument is 30.48 metres tall and is modelled on the first Eddystone Lighthouse. Sir John Barrow was born in humble circumstances at a local cottage in Dragley Beck, and rose to the high position of Permanent Secretary to the Admiralty.

The market town of Ulverston is celebrated for the legendary Ulverstonian, Stan Laurel, whose real name was Arthur Stanley Jefferson. He was born on 16 June 1890 in his grandparent's house at No 3 Argyle Street and became world famous for his films with Oliver Hardy. The world's only museum devoted to Laurel and Hardy is now to be found in the auditorium of the Roxy Cinema, Brogden Street, Ulverston, near the railway station, an appropriate 1930s venue where films are still shown on the big screen. So why not go along to see the classic 1930s film *Sons of the Desert*

A view of Ulverston station from the footplate of 'A4' 4-6-2 No 4498 *Sir Nigel Gresley* on 2 August 1979. *Peter Fitton*

and examine the museum collection devoted to the comedy duo? Close by, a statue to the famous duo may be seen outside Coronation Hall.

Ulverston is a convenient centre for exploring the Lake District and the Furness peninsula, and there are plenty of surprises nearby. For example, Conishead Priory is a spectacular building within walking distance of Ulverston station. It was founded by Gamel de Pennington, with the consent of the Baron of Kendal in the reign of Henry II. On its dissolution in the reign of Henry VIII, it was claimed by the King as Duke of Lancaster. In 1821 Colonel Thomas Richard Gale Braddyll commenced building the modern-day priory, and in 1874 it was bought by John Poole, a local solicitor. In 1878 he sold the priory and the surrounding park of around 150 acres to a Scottish syndicate, and it was converted to a spa hotel, which became a popular destination until at least the turn of the century. Nowadays the priory is known as the Manjushri Kadampa Buddhist Centre. It and the Buddhist temple are open to the public with guided tours led by a member of the Buddhist community. The Furness line is very well known among Buddhists, and on certain dates Ulverston station is full of crimson-robed devotees from all over the world.

Away from quiet contemplation inside the Kadampa Temple for world peace and back on track to the north of Ulverston, the railway takes a curvaceous route through two substantial deep cuttings. Ascending to the 78.9-metre summit at the highest point of the Furness line, the double track plunges into Lindal Tunnel. In the regular days of steam, northbound trains had to work very hard ascending the 1 in 80 Lindal Bank, with heavy freight trains requiring a banking engine. Lindal once had its own station, but it

Above: The Grade II-listed Italianate Ulverston station was built in 1874 and is one of the finest preserved stations on the line, with an unusual island platform and high clock tower. Class 185 No 185129 leaves forming a Barrow to Manchester Airport service on 17 January 2009. *Mark Bartlett*

Right: The Furness Railway monogram is artistically incorporated into a lamp at Ulverston station. *Peter Fitton*

closed on 1 October 1951. Today Lindal Bank is favoured by photographers as a prime location for dramatic photographs of steam specials.

Significantly, the Lindal area was once firmly associated with the iron ore industry, which gave birth to the Furness Railway in 1846. Lindale's most famous resident was John Wilkinson, an ironworker and inventor who lived in the village from 1750. He produced the iron for the world's first iron bridge at Ironbridge and made the

world's first iron boat in 1787. An obelisk stands in the village as a memorial to him.

The line now reaches the medieval town of Dalton-in-Furness. The ancient capital of Furness existed long before Barrow emerged with the coming of the railway. The town boasts a number of historic buildings, particularly along Market Street, Church Street and Market Place, as well as interesting specialist shops, and holds a street market on Tuesdays all year round. Dalton Castle, a 14th-century peel

castle, overlooks the town and was latterly a place where manorial courts were held. The origin of the parish church, too, is of medieval origin, circa 1181, though the present church is built upon the old foundations. Dalton was the home of the painter George Romney (1734-1802) and he is buried in the churchyard of St Mary's parish church. After Dalton the train enters the 203-metre-long Dalton Tunnel and shortly thereafter the Barrow avoiding line diverges to the right at Dalton Junction.

The next station was formerly Furness Abbey, built adjacent to the Furness Abbey Hotel, with a covered walkway connecting the two. The station was under the supervision of a top-hatted station master during the era of Alfred Aslett, but it closed on 25 September 1950 and both hotel and station are now demolished.

Furness Abbey is located in the 'Vale of Nightshade', a natural amphitheatre south of Dalton-in-Furness. The former monastery dates back to 1123 and was once the second wealthiest and most powerful Cistercian monastery in the country. Its monks were large land-owners, and built Piel Castle to control trade between the Furness peninsula and the Isle of Man. The abbey passed to

SR 4-6-0 No 850 *Lord Nelson* makes the gruelling ascent of Lindal Bank with the down 'Cumbrian Coast Express' on 2 September 1979. *Peter Fitton*

the Cistercians in 1147, who gradually enlarged and rebuilt the ornate church. By the 15th century it had been completely remodelled and had become the second richest and most powerful – as well as one of the grandest – Cistercian abbeys in England.

The monks occasionally found themselves between the regularly warring Scots and English. The abbey was destroyed in 1537 during the English Reformation under the order of Henry VIII; about 300 monks resided within its walls, but by the time of Henry's dissolution of the monasteries only 33 were left to surrender to the King's commissioners.

The awesome ruin is, of course, best seen at close quarters, and visitors cannot fail to be impressed by its grandeur and history and the conceptions it may bring to mind. With time to reflect, one can imagine a ghostly scene with visions of white men in white habits roaming up and down the extensive grounds.

The penultimate station before reaching Barrow-in-Furness is Roose, a growing suburb of Barrow. Here one can disembark from the train for Furness Abbey. Alternatively, enjoy a nice walk to the Furness peninsula to discover the archipelago of Furness islands incorporating Foulney, Piel and Roa islands. A heritage walk along the old trackbed of the Furness branch line from Cavendish Dock to

Above: The ruins of Furness Abbey may be observed from the carriage window on the right shortly after passing through a short tunnel. *Neal Hardy*

Right: A charming photograph of Furness Abbey station, now sadly demolished. *Bob Gregson railway archive*

Rampside and the site of the station on Roa Island is described later –Walk 4.

It was the Furness Railway that once provided the wheels of industry at Barrow's Hindpool Iron Works and four docks – Devonshire, Buccleuch, Cavendish and Ramsden – the latter bearing the name of Sir James Ramsden. Barrow-in-Furness has played a vital role in global ship and submarine construction for more than 125 years. The shipyard grew to become the principal industry of Barrow using locally manufactured steel from Barrow Iron Works, thus the two industries became interdependent.

Vickers Shipbuilding & Engineering Ltd originally built all types of ships, the notable list including 373 merchant ships, 312 submarines and 148 naval surface ships. All but three of the Royal Navy's nuclear submarines were built in Barrow, as well as the current Royal Navy flagship HMS *Bulwark*. Two notable big ships I recollect seeing under construction here were the passenger liner *Oriana* for P&O and the aircraft carrier HMS *Invincible*.

Rail access to Ramsden Dock at the southern end of Barrow Island involved crossing the Buccleuch Dock bridge, but closure of the bridge in 1967 on safety grounds led to the end of the dock's railways. Nowadays the once extensive network has disappeared with the exception of rusty single-track link to the main line at Salthouse Junction. The docks themselves see little commercial activity other than the occasional ship with its nuclear cargo destined to travel by rail to Sellafield. The parent company's shipbuilding division is now BAE Systems Submarine Solutions.

The industry is now concentrated on the building of nuclear submarines for the Royal Navy, including the controversial Trident. They are built in Cumbria's tallest building, 51 metres high and designed to prevent satellite surveillance. The colossal Devonshire Dock Hall was completed in 1986 and was built on land created by

Piel Island and its ruined castle is a well-known Barrow landmark. Approaching Barrow, it may be glimpsed from the train across Cavendish Dock. *Neal Hardy*

infilling part of Devonshire Dock. The building is a familiar landmark and is visible from the train from afar as it rounds Morecambe Bay and the Duddon estuary.

Departing from Barrow-in-Furness, the track is reduced to a single line that extends to the junction with the Barrow avoiding line at Park South Junction. The avoiding line is double track and rejoins the main line south of Askham station. It is mainly used by freight and special trains and is about 1 mile in length. By contrast, the Barrow loop, serving Roose and Barrow, is used by all service passenger trains but is more than 8 miles long. After the junction the train arrives at Askam station, another Austin & Paley design that has unfortunately seen better days.

The Duddon Sands now come into view. The sands and mudflats are the haunt of oystercatcher, redshank, heron, shelduck and curlew, which may on occasions be observed from the train as it rounds the bay. At this point it only seems a stone's throw across the estuary to Millom. The lofty spire of St George's church dominates the skyline, though to reach that Millom landmark will take another 10 miles around three sides of the Duddon estuary.

It is therefore little wonder that during the 19th century there were plans to bridge the estuary between Askam and Millom, but they were aborted, and materials stockpiled on the banks of the Duddon near the rocky outcrop of Dunnerholme are testament to a failed Victorian enterprise. Askam-in-Furness was once dominated by iron-smelting furnaces, though today there is little evidence of its industrial origins apart from the remnants of slag heaps close to the railway. Leaving Askam-in-Furness we pass Kirkby-in-Furness, where the Furness Railway had its origins in 1846, serving the slate-quarrying industry. To this day slate is still being cut at the huge quarries high up on the slopes of Kirkby Moor.

DMU No 156479 arrives at Barrow-in-Furness on 28 April 2014. *Mark Bartlett*

At Foxfield station the island platform still has a unique wooden signal box; it was once attached to the station buildings, which included a trainshed. Nearby the cast-iron water tower remains as a last vestige of the age of steam. To this day I imagine the ghost of the cheery-faced porter on Foxfield platform chanting 'Foxfield, change here for Broughton and Coniston', all long ago closed but not forgotten.

The Furness line now rounds the estuary via the sharp Foxfield curve near where the Coniston branch diverged. It then crosses over a third low-level viaduct spanning

Class 'B1' *Mayflower* and 'V2' *Green Arrow* double-head southwards past Foxfield on the lovely summer afternoon of 21 June 1975. *David Hindle*

the River Duddon. This river has its source high up in the hills of the Wrynose Pass, and a walk in the picturesque Duddon Valley is well worthwhile. The Duddon estuary nestles beneath the rounded outline of Black Combe, and approaching Green Road station the line passes meadows thick with buttercups. Inland there are nationally important raised bogs designated as Sites

Class 5 No 45134 heads the SLS/MLS Furness Railway tour near Park South on the Barrow avoiding line on 2 September 1967. *Peter Fitton*

of Special Scientific Interest. Salt marshes and mudflats may be reached from the next isolated unstaffed halt.

That Green Road, formerly known as Underhill, somehow managed to escape the Beeching 'axe' is something of an enigma. Another puzzle is the Swinside Stone Circle, which may be reached from the station.

After Green Road the train reaches the small Cumbrian town of Millom, situated on the south-west tip of the old county of Cumberland. The Lakeland poet and author Norman Nicholson was born and bred here; a blue plaque marks No 14 St George's Terrace, where he resided for

most of his working life. One of his books all about Millom is titled *Wednesday Early Closing*, so let his endearing title serve as a reminder that it still is. Alight here for Millom town centre and the Hodbarrow Nature Reserve (Walk 6).

You need a well-trained eye to spot the course of a mineral branch line that once veered off from sidings at Millom station to serve Millom ironworks and the Hodbarrow mines. Their closure in 1968 led to the loss of a substantial amount of freight for the Furness line. Also lost was an interesting collection of industrial steam engines, including the incredible steam crane affectionately known as 'Snipey'.

Silecroft station is a request stop: trains are summoned to stop by passengers giving a clear hand signal to the driver or by telling the guard of an intention to disembark. The line still has the feeling of a branch line and a community spirit, so typical of the pre-Beeching era, with the train stopping at wayside halts and old-fashioned stations. Complete with a Class 37 diesel locomotive of the 1980s upfront, it rekindles many memories of the branch-line era.

Black Combe's rugged grandeur can now be seen at close quarters from the carriage window. You can make the ascent of this lone sentinel, which stands at around 600 metres high, from Silecroft station (Walk

Left: A Derby lightweight diesel multiple unit forming an up local service calls at Green Road station near Millom on 2 September 1967. *Peter Fitton*

Right: 'Snipey' the wee steam crane. *David Eaves*

Millom Iron Works shed, complete with its own fleet of saddle tanks. *David Hindle*

Approaching Silecroft, 'Sir Nigel, you have the road! *David Hindle'*

7). Alternatively, why not enjoy a relaxing walk to the surprisingly sandy beach? A pair of binoculars is recommended to observe the summit of Snaefell on the Isle of Man, or even to watch flocks of gannet (our largest seabird) plunging into the sea to catch and devour the mackerel shoals.

Not only is this line abounding in coastal scenery, but between Silecroft and Ravenglass it also passes through the Lake District National Park, which is one of the most popular areas in the country, attracting visitors from all over the world. Set against a backdrop of mountains, lakes, woodlands, rivers, picturesque villages and sublime scenery, there is so much to delight the visitor within its bounds.

The Bootle station area, situated about a mile from the village of that name, grew up as a community in its own right and today is simply known by locals as Bootle Station, as distinct from Bootle itself. Although now a residential dwelling, the station building, signal box and warehouse have survived almost unaltered since the railway was built. However, the station narrowly missed a cataclysmic disaster on 22 March 1945 when a goods train travelling south with a wagonload of depth charges caught fire. The signalman endeavoured to stop traffic on the line but it was the heroic action of the train crew that prevented a greater disaster. Fireman Norman Stubbs, then aged 23 years, bravely uncoupled the wagon from the rest of the train. The driver pulled forward and Stubbs went to put detonators on the opposite line as there was a troop train due. He had only placed one or two detonators when the wagon exploded and he was thrown through the air and knocked unconscious. For his actions he was awarded the George Medal for bravery and the Order of Industrial Heroism. The explosion

Above: Preserved 'A4' 4-6-2 No 4498 *Sir Nigel Gresley* heads the down 'Cumbrian Coast Express' at Silecroft on 2 August 1979. *David Hindle*

Right: Preserved BR Standard 4-6-2 No 71000 *Duke of Gloucester* hauls the 'Cumbrian Coast Express' past Whitbeck on the lower reaches of Black Combe between Silecroft and Bootle on 28 October 1986. *Peter Fitton*

blew a crater 50 feet deep, and tragically the driver, Harold Goodall, was killed.

A few kilometres north of Bootle, on the seaward side at Eskmeals, we pass the Eskmeals Qinetic Armaments Testing Range. Top secret, no doubt, though the sand dunes adjacent to it fringing the River Esk form part of an important botanical site; the Eskmeal's Nature Reserve is there to be enjoyed by everyone.

Inland the landscape is enhanced by the historic Muncaster Castle, which is prominently situated on the crest of a wooded hill overlooking the River Esk. It may be reached from Ravenglass station about a mile away. The castle is owned by the Pennington family, successive generations of whom have resided here for at least 800 years. The Muncaster estate was granted to Alan de Penitone in 1208, and the castle was built in 1258 on the foundations of a previous Roman settlement. Its original purpose was as a fortress to defend against the Scots, but it was later used as an outpost protecting the trade routes from

Carlisle. The oldest parts include the Great Hall and the 14th-century peel tower. However, be aware that Muncaster Castle is one of Britain's most haunted buildings; scientists have been researching the castle's ghosts since 1992 and are still unable to explain some of the strange occurrences reported there.

During May and June the gardens and woodlands on the estate are a blaze of colour, with an abundance of azaleas and rhododendrons. Within the woodlands there is an owl sanctuary, and if you are told to 'get lost' head for the maze! Muncaster's gardens include features

designed to take advantage of the lovely views of the Lakeland hills and the valley of the Esk, with its distinctive railway viaduct.

The first wooden railway viaduct constructed over the Esk was badly damaged by fire in 1856, and it has been rebuilt several times since, the most recent reconstruction being in 1984. Depending on the season and state of the tide, look out for a range of interesting wildfowl and waders while crossing. At Ravenglass two rivers, the Esk and the Mite, converge into an estuary on the Irish Sea.

Ravenglass is the Lake District National Park's only coastal village. It was once an important Roman naval base and parts of the Roman bath house are still standing. The northern shore of the estuary at Drigg Point was once the largest black-headed gullery in Europe. There was also a thriving sandwich tern colony, but since the late 1970/80s it has been completely forsaken as a breeding colony by both species.

Ravenglass station is now the Ratty Arms pub, where there is a railway interchange with the historic Ravenglass & Eskdale Railway. Appropriately three of the much-admired

A Class 153 unit pauses at Bootle station on 27 July 2013 en route to Carlisle. *Mark Bartlett*

veteran R&ER steam engines, resplendent in bright colours and in immaculate condition, are named after their namesake local rivers, *Esk*, *Irt* and *Mite*.

In 1875 the 3-foot-gauge Ravenglass & Eskdale Railway first penetrated the hills and valleys of West Cumberland for iron ore mined at Boot, and opened for passengers on 20 November 1876. The 'La'al Ratty', as it is affectionately known, has been integrated into the Lakeland landscape and is now a tourist line, providing immense pleasure to countless hordes of people as it threads its way up the Eskdale valley.

A few metres north of the station the fifth of the distinctive major viaducts of the Furness Railway crosses the River Mite. Typical birds of the estuary that may be observed from the Esk and Mite viaducts on the intertidal mud flats may include shelduck, wigeon, mallard, teal, heron, oystercatcher, redshank, curlew and little egret.

The next station, Drigg, might be described, to use an eloquent term, as the 'arse end of nowhere'. Moreover, it has the distinction of being a 'low-level waste repository' – a euphemism for a nuclear dump – which is served by a line that veers off to the left to the 'no-go' top-secret site! Before that it was the site of ROF Drigg, built in 1940 to manufacture TNT (trinitrotulence); the remote location was chosen because the factory manufactured high explosives. At this point I avoid looking left and look landward to observe Scafell, England's highest mountain, and the mountain range of the western Lake District.

Above left: LMS 'Jubilee' Class No 5690 *Leander* crosses Eskmeals Viaduct on 4 September 1979. *Peter Fitton*

Left: An unidentified diesel multiple unit crosses the River Mite Viaduct at Ravenglass. There are six architecturally distinctive low viaducts along the course of the Furness line spanning the estuaries of the rivers Kent, Levens, Duddon, Esk, Mite and Irt. *Bob Gregson railway archive*

The next station, Seascale, is situated above the shore of the Irish Sea where the mountains form a sheltering backdrop to the lowland rolling pastures of West Cumbria. In Victorian times it was a popular seaside resort for visitors who arrived by train from northern England to enjoy the golden sands and safe sea bathing. It was envisaged that it would develop as a major tourist resort, but this was not to materialise.

At Sellafield, the huge nuclear plant dominates the landscape and is operated by Sellafield Ltd on behalf of the Nuclear Decommissioning Authority. Despite industrial contraction elsewhere along the Cumbrian coast, the railway connection to the Sellafield plant regenerated the Cumbrian Coast Line, with many workers commuting to the site. Essential freight trains convey nuclear material from power stations throughout the country and from abroad. Under the Beeching proposals there is little doubt that the central section of the Cumbrian Coast Line from Barrow to Whitehaven would have closed but

Seascale is the station for Wastwater, which nowadays can only be reached by cycle, car or taxi, there being no public transport to what is surely the most breathtaking of Britain's lakes. *Neal Hardy*

for the nuclear plant. There is usually an interesting assortment of DRS diesel locomotives stabled here.

Sellafield used to be the junction for the Furness Railway's loop line to Whitehaven, serving Beckermet and Egremont, but its course is now but a scar on the landscape.

Leaving Sellafield, the current main line is reduced to a single track for 11 miles to Whitehaven, barring a passing loop at St Bees. At times this superlative coastal stretch seems to be almost on the beach, where cormorants perch in small flocks hanging out their wings to dry, and a few grey seals haul out on the shingle. The train passes the tiny coastal halts of Braystones and Nethertown, where very few trains stop. One wonders if Dr Beeching really knew about stations like these and others serving small settlements along the line. Did the corridors of Whitehall fail him or was he in complete denial?

There are spectacular views as we journey northwards, with the Isle of Man visible across the Irish Sea on a clear day. From the train I have witnessed the contrasts of both tempestuous seas and golden sands lapped by azure waters shimmering in the sunshine. You will see much evidence of the Energy Coast, with hundreds of huge wind turbines and gas platforms far out to sea contrasting with the

On 17 October 2013 Class 37s Nos 37608 and 37682 are seen at Grange powering the morning flask train from Crewe to Sellafield. *Mark Bartlett*

small shanty homesteads beside the railway. The foregoing factors contribute to the allure of a railway journey, which at times is not dissimilar to the route of the famous 'Cornish Rivera Express'.

On exposed sections of the single line between Sellafield and St Bees, Whitehaven and Workington, Network Rail receives weather warnings from the

Met Office. This is to prepare for the possibility of the sea breaching coastal defences at times of high tides and storm conditions. Network Rail also relies on reports from drivers about worsening weather conditions and obviously in the worst possible scenario the line is closed, we hope!

St Bees is served by its own station and

is noteworthy for its former Benedictine church and the famous grammar school, founded in 1587 by Archbishop Grindall. Legend has it that St Bees takes its name from an Irish nun, St Bega, who founded a small nunnery here in the 7th century, after escaping from Ireland, when a forced marriage to a Norse chieftain was planned. The land, on a 3-mile stretch around the headland, was granted to her by Lord Egremont after he told her, in midsummer, that she could have as much land as was covered by snow. The next day it snowed and she was granted the land.

Close to St Bees station in Main Street a new museum devoted entirely to the Furness Railway has been established by Peter Rooke in the old village police station. The museum holds thousands of interesting and historical exhibits dating from 1840 and is well worth a visit.

St Bees has a long sandy beach, with refreshment facilities. St Bees Head is an RSPB nature reserve with a thriving seabird colony where puffins are occasionally seen. It is notable as being England's only breeding site for the black guillemot, which nests around Fleswick Bay. Alight here for the starting point of the Coast to Coast walk and St Bees Head (Walk 8).

To the north of St Bees station the line swings inland through pleasant countryside to reach Corkickle, where the rural landscape changes dramatically, with constant reminders of West Cumbria's industrial inheritance. On 31 October 1986 Albright & Wilson Limited closed the unique Corkickle Brake Incline, which was formerly visible from the train at Corkickle. It was reputed to be the last commercially operated standard-gauge cable-worked incline in Britain. Close by at Whitehaven the Howgill Brake linked Whitehaven harbour with the Haig Pit. The Howgill Brake was situated on the site of an 18th-century wagonway until it was realigned in 1923 to cope with the coal from the new Haig Colliery; this was the last of the deep coal mines in Cumbria and it marked the end of an era when it closed in 1986.

At St Bees station on 11 September 1974 Class 25 No 25041 stands on the down line as classmate No 25114 approaches with an up freight. Note the tablet exchange for single-line working. *Peter Fitton*

The single-track Bransty Tunnel between Corkickle and Whitehaven Bransty stations is the longest on the line at 1,219 metres, and was completed in 1852. At Whitehaven the Furness Railway station was demolished in 1981 and replaced with the insensitive construction we see there today. Whitehaven was once one of England's busiest ports and was attacked by the pirate John Paul Jones in 1778. The

Right: Steam operations ceased on Whitehaven's colliery rail network on 1 March 1975. Thereafter the future of the local coal-mining industry and Ladysmith Colliery (illustrated) remained uncertain. *Peter Fitton*

Above: Giesl ejector-fitted *Repulse* rests in Ladysmith Colliery shed, Whitehaven, on 11 April 1974. I remember the shed and its occupants well. *Peter Fitton*

Left: Harrington's *Warspite* was one of two Austerity 0-6-0STs that worked at the Harrington coal preparation plant before it closed, when they were transferred to Whitehaven's Ladysmith Colliery. This loco was fitted with the narrow Giesl ejector funnel but sister engine *Amazon* had a standard chimney. Driver Raymond Penn, formerly a BR fireman at Carlisle Upperby, is seen in charge of *Warspite* as it goes about its arduous duties. *David Hindle*

Left: Something has caught the eye of these workers at Whitehaven Harbour as the NCB's Barclay 0-4-0ST No 8 simmers on the quayside at the bottom of the Howgill Brake during its twilight years in 1968. Although it continued to be busy for some time thereafter, the coal traffic and the rails are now long gone. *David Hindle*

Below left: Peckett 0-4-0ST *Victoria*, built as Works No 2028/1942 for the Royal Ordnance Factory at Sellafield, is seen here being watered outside the Quaker Oats building at Whitehaven Harbour in 1968. It worked at the harbour for a further three years. *David Hindle*

Below: This busy scene alongside the harbour at Whitehaven in 1968 features two 0-4-0ST locomotives, Peckett *Victoria* on the left and a numberless and unnamed Robert Stephenson Hawthorn locomotive, believed to date from 1942, on the right. *David Hindle*

ancient harbour is now a marina where the Beacon Visitor Centre is situated.

Whitehaven Harbour also once had an extensive rail network and its own fleet of steam locomotives. During the heyday of the bustling harbour they would shunt trucks full of coal, iron, gypsum and many other cargoes onto the quays for ships to take elsewhere in the world. The accompanying photographs were taken in 1968 and show the last of the industrial steam at work within the precincts of the harbour shortly before their withdrawal.

Whitehaven marks the end of the Furness Railway, but the coast-hugging route continues as a single track for 7 miles via Parton and Harrington to Workington. Though spectacular, the latter section of track is particularly vulnerable to a combination of high tides and winter storms. From Workington the Cumbrian Coast Line continues north to Maryport with good views of the Solway Firth and a backdrop of Criffel straddling the Scottish coast. After Maryport the line swings eastwards and leaves the coast towards Carlisle, serving Aspatria, Wigton and Dalston. The 105-mile train journey from Carnforth to Carlisle takes nearly 4 hours and there are up to 34 intermediate stations and request stops.

At the northern end of the line is the city of Carlisle. Nearby is the border with Scotland, while to the east lie the remains of the famous Roman wall, now a World Heritage Site. Carlisle has had a tumultuous history, which is mirrored in its castle where Mary Queen of Scots was once confined. The castle now houses Cumbria's military museum and, together with the magnificent Cathedral and the Tullis House Museum, is well worth a visit.

From Carlisle it is possible to make a very interesting round trip back to Lancaster via the famous Settle to Carlisle line, changing at Skipton. The fascination and allure of this route are enduring and I have travelled it on many memorable occasions. On 14 February 2017 diagrammed steam returned to the railway network for the first time since 3 August 1968, and featured the reinvented 'A1' 4-6-2 *Tornado* making a series of timetabled workings on the Settle to Carlisle line between Appleby and Skipton.

Carlisle is, of course, a major transport hub with links to Newcastle, Edinburgh, Glasgow, Leeds, Manchester, Birmingham and London, and was once served by no fewer than six pre-Grouping railway companies: the London & North Western, Maryport & Carlisle, Midland, North Eastern, Glasgow & South Western, North British, and Caledonian. Accordingly, getting home should not have presented a problem when exploring the Cumbrian coast by rail.

See Chapter 13 for a list of birdwatching and heritage walks, including those mentioned in this chapter.

Carlisle station has long been a railway hub. *Bob Gregson railway archive*

Route map of the Cumbrian Coast Railway and associated lines (open and closed)

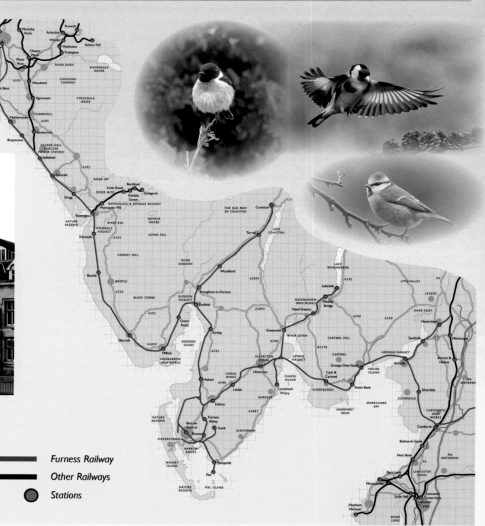

Above: A view of the splendid frontage of Carlisle station at 10.06 on 7 August 1990. For many visitors a starting point for a journey southwards on the Cumbrian coast line. Readers will no doubt recall many of the vehicle types seen in this image from almost thirty years ago. *Peter Butler/Silver Link Archive*

(Captions and credits for the wildlife images can be found in the following pages)

Furness Railway

Other Railways

Stations

5 A railway for pleasure: memories of the Furness Railway

This chapter is different in that it is partly anecdotal, combining research with miscellaneous memorabilia. In it I revisit people and places and unrelated bizarre happenings along the Furness line with an underlying theme of pleasure. More than half a century before the first motor cars emerged, the coming of the railway made everything 'all change'. The people of Furness and West Cumbria became less isolated with easier access to the Lake District, increased leisure time and greater social mobility. With more time to spare at weekends, they gradually came to depend upon the passenger service for work and leisure, and as a means to reach far-flung destinations. It gave passengers the freedom to visit relatives and go on holiday or into town to do some shopping. The line has always been used for the conveyance of freight as well as the conveyance of schoolchildren and tourists and all-encompassing business travel in the broadest sense of the word.

The emergence of the earliest music halls coincided with the advent of the first railways, including the Furness Railway, and the relationship between them is one of the most striking features of Victorian social history.

'Let's all go to the music hall'

The Furness Railway has long been a vehicle for pleasure and enjoyment and has served the popular entertainment industry. In the mid-19th century it was the railways that lured the public to the theatres and other places of entertainment. It provided new horizons for all classes of people, including travellers from far and wide who enjoyed the coming of the first music halls, cinemas, circuses and concert halls to the region. Corresponding with the development of the railway network, the earliest music halls and theatres of the Victorian era began to feature international performances on a lavish scale, increasingly served by the railway with improved mobility for scenery, costumes, animals and equipment. Theatre groups and their crews toured the provinces, as did renowned music hall performers. The Furness Railway came to be used by the promoters of pleasure and as a foundation for cultural enjoyment, and by those engaged in music hall and the popular entertainment industry. Favourable terms were offered by the Furness Railway for travelling music hall artists during 1897:

'On or after 1st October 1897, parties of music hall artists and their assistants, numbering five persons and upwards, will be conveyed distances above 20 miles at the undermentioned rate: single journey – three-fourths of the ordinary single fare, return journey – ordinary single fare and one half. The tickets to be made available until the end of the tour; ordinary paper tickets will be issued to stations, endorsed music hall artists; only one half the ordinary cloakroom charges are to be made to music hall artists. Luggage will be a minimum of one penny per package.'

The first tramcars and omnibuses were not only an important stimulus to the social and economic development of the outer suburbs of towns like Barrow. They also meant that the public could now attend out-of-town entertainment. By the 1920s some of those residing in rural parishes and villages along the line would have been eager to catch a train into town to see the latest live shows or the silent flickering pictures that were to be succeeded by the talkies in the 1930s. During the cinema boom of the 1940s and '50s most towns and seaside resorts had their own cinemas, from the Roxy Cinema at Carnforth to the Ritz and the Palladium at Millom. At Whitehaven there used to be three cinemas – the Gaiety, the Queens, and the Empire – now consigned to history. At Barrow-in-Furness there was a wealth of cinemas to choose from including the Coliseum, Electric Theatre, Essoldo, Hippodrome, Pavilion, Ritz, Roxy, Royalty and the Tivoli Music Hall (formerly the Alexandra) on Forshaw Street, which opened in 1867. Her Majesty's Theatre was the last commercial theatre to close in the town in 1973.

Alfred Aslett provides further evidence as to how the Furness Railway was used for pleasure in the late Victorian and Edwardian era in a 1916 publication.

'It is sufficient to say that the claims of sport are generously recognised, and golfers, anglers, etc. may obtain cheap special day tickets; that the pleasure resorts on the line are open all the year round, at fares approaching single fares for the double journey.'

Certain changes in working class culture were to have an effect on life styles and attitudes towards popular entertainment to be enjoyed by railway passengers. An examination of the diaries of the renowned contralto Kathleen Ferrier shows that she used the railway network while residing at Carlisle at the beginning of her career, and at Silloth until 1940. In wartime Britain she travelled throughout Cumberland bringing music to the factories, villages and other establishments, before heading to London and gaining international fame.

The lost train of Lindal

The music halls regularly featured twice-nightly performances where comedy was a vital part of the repertoire. Certain stories concerning the Furness Railway would not have been out of place on the music hall stage.

At the height of the music hall era on 22 September 1892, 0-6-0 locomotive No 115 was quietly engaged in shunting a few quarry wagons when the earth beneath it suddenly parted company with the track. On seeing some rather ominous cracks precipitously appearing in the ground, the crew managed to leap from the footplate, but the locomotive toppled over the brink with a one-way ticket into the vast hole, where it remains for eternity as a relic of railway heritage, albeit 200 feet below the surface of the earth at Lindal. The driver subsequently reported the matter to his superiors and the police, to whom he explained: 'I seem to have lost my engine but at least it was given a decent burial.' RIP No 115. This account is perhaps a poignant reminder of subsidence, a short distance from the portal of Lindal Tunnel near Dalton-in-Furness, so I think the message is to travel light!

'I seem to have lost my engine, but at least it was given a good burial. RIP No 115.' *Cartoon by David Eaves*

'You're drunk, sir – here, let me drive, my good man.' *Cartoon by David Eaves*

'A driver in liquor'

Next on the bill, it is on record that the driver of one of the first passenger trains was found to be totally inebriated. Unfortunately for him, this was witnessed and documented by his boss, the first Locomotive Superintendent, Mr James Ramsden, then only 23 years old, who took over driving the engine. (In later years he went on to achieve distinction in Barrow as the town's first Mayor, and was later knighted.) In 1890 Sir James recalled the incident:

'In 1846 passengers were allowed to travel in a sheep van fitted by a carpenter with neat deal seats. I observed one Sunday that the engine was running fast and, making signals for the train to stop, I found the driver in liquor. I afterwards wrote to the Superintendent of the Manchester to Liverpool Railway and begged a man and, until his arrival, which was not for some days, I worked the traffic myself.'

Henry Schneider and entourage take the Lakeside train

One of the most famous of the regular travellers on the Ulverston to Lakeside branch line during Victorian times was Henry Schneider, a prosperous industrialist and cofounder of the Furness Railway. In 1869, while Chairman of the Barrow Steelworks, he bought Belsfield House, situated on an island at Bowness-on-Windermere. Every morning he left his palatial residence preceded by his butler, who carried a heated silver salver at a discreet distance ahead of his master. This distinctively odd procession continued until

FR No 20, seen here at Haverthwaite on 22 August 2000, would in all probability have been familiar to Henry Schneider during the late 19th century as he journeyed to work along the Lakeside branch. *Peter Fitton*

they boarded Schneider's twin-screw steam yacht *Esperance* to sail the tranquil waters of Windermere for 6 miles to Lakeside railway station. During the sail the butler served his master with an extravagant gourmet breakfast from the silver salver. At Lakeside, after devouring the gastronomic delight, Schneider transferred from steam yacht to steam train and travelled the Lakeside branch in his own private compartment to arrive at his office at the steelworks.

Schneider died at Belsfield on 11 November 1887, aged 72. The TSSY *Esperance* is preserved at the Windermere Jetty (Steamboat Museum) and is said to be the model for the houseboat in Arthur Ransome's novel *Swallows and Amazons*.

FR No 20 and Victorian admirers pose at Haverthwaite station on the same day, another scene that would have been vaguely familiar to Henry Schneider. *Peter Fitton*

'Pack Up Your Troubles in Your Old Kit-Bag'

There are, of course, many elements of social history concerning the Furness Railway, and not all are happy ones. It should be remembered that the railway also had an important role to play throughout the sorrow and heartache of two World Wars. The First World War saw the last stand of music hall exuberance, and Florrie Forde boosted morale with the rallying song written in 1915, 'Pack Up Your Troubles in Your Old Kit-Bag, and Smile, Smile, Smile'.

The Union Jack probably fluttered in the breeze as a series of speakers underlined Earl Kitchener's immortal plea of 'England Needs You' to supplement the British Expeditionary Force in France. In 1915 recruitment drives were held for local men to join the armed forces, and my Grandfather Bowman, residing at Askam with Ireleth near Barrow, was one such recruit who answered the call and boarded the train at Millom to enrol for active service on 2 March 1916. Private Rowland Bowman served his country in the Machine Gun Regiment at the infamous Battle of Ypres. The corps was formed in October 1915 in response to the need for more effective use of machine guns on the Western Front, but poignantly it was also

thousands of troops off to war, while the local Home Guard kept a ceaseless watch for German paratroopers.

The Fuhrer's Blitz on Barrow-in Furness came on the nights of 14-16 April and 3-10 May 1941. Houses surrounding the principal industries took the bulk of the bombing and 83 people were killed and more than 300 were injured. The difficulty in targeting bombs meant that the shipyards and steelworks were often missed, at the expense of residential areas. The shipyard was targeted and Barrow Central station was destroyed.

Also hit was an ornate gazebo housing locomotive No 3 *Coppernob*, which had been displayed at the station following its retirement in 1907. After the war Barrow station was completely rebuilt incorporating the Furness Railway's War Memorial to its employees killed in the First World War.

'Millom Rejoices'

The following extract from the *Millom Gazette* reporting on Armistice Day, 11 November 1918, under the heading 'Millom Rejoices', illustrates how the railway featured in the celebrations:

'Rumours were current in the town before nine o'clock that the armistice had been

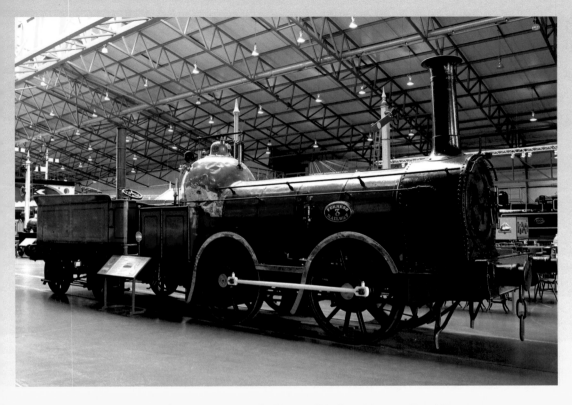

Furness Railway No 3 *Coppernob* in retirement at the National Railway Museum. *David Eaves*

known as the 'suicide club'. The so-called Great War led to a terrible loss of life, which included many local brave soldiers who died on the battlefields of northern France.

Throughout both World Wars the railway was of strategic importance in serving Barrow's naval construction yards and Messrs Vickers gun-making plant at Eskmeals. The Furness Railway also carried

signed at 5a.m. but no official news was forthcoming. The first definite confirmation of the fact came through from Station Master Ware, who got the intelligence from the railway authorities. Then Millom burst with one accord with a display of bunting, flags shot through windows everywhere and lines of streamers were soon hung across the streets… Everywhere delighted faces were to be seen, and a joyous procession of Vickers employees, who had promptly obtained a holiday, came pouring out of the railway station; the girls with their breasts bedecked with small Union Jacks and the national colours, linking arms with each other and with male companions, sang their way homeward, many of them dancing as well.'

Millom: a forgotten Cumbrian town with plenty of memories

Millom is steeped in local history and industrial archaeology. The small town nestles in a sublime landscape alongside the Duddon estuary against a backdrop of the south-west Cumbrian mountains and overshadowed by the landmark of Black Combe. There are neat rows of terraced houses and period shops in streets buzzing with the friendly people of this tight-knit community, perhaps reminiscent of 'Coronation Street'.

Millom Iron Works was the town's principal employer until its closure in 1968. The views of the estuary across to Sandscale, Dunnerholme, Walney Island and the mountains of south-west Cumbria are something to behold, yet they are only a short distance from Millom as the seagull flies. While travelling by train around the Duddon estuary the sight of the prominent spire of Millom's St George's church reawakens memories of the concept of a failed Victorian railway initiative and a forgotten Cumbrian town

My ancestors residing in Millom occasionally used the railway for pleasure. My great uncle Barker Clarke began his working life in Millom's Hodbarrow mine and his story broadly parallels the growth and prosperity of the Furness Railway. My grandma – old nan – Winifrid Jane Bloomfontein Clarke, known as 'Tein', was raised at Borwick Rails, Millom, in the shadow of the ironworks. Her father, William Edward Clarke, joined the Coldstream Guards in 1891 and served with them for 12 years, spending three years in South Africa.

It seems that the smart dress uniform of the Coldstream Guards caught my great-grandmother Sophrona's eye, and they married at Kensington Register Office in 1898. The family moved to Millom Newtown, where a rich seam of haematite had been discovered. William Edward was stationed in Bloemfontein when his daughter Winifred Jane, my grandmother, was born, and he wrote to his new wife while serving in the Boer War, suggesting that his daughter should be named after the town where he had been stationed.

Born and bred in Millom, 'Tein', her parents and nine brothers and sisters

A striking image of William Edward Clarke fighting for his country on horseback during the Boar War of 1899-1902. His daughter, Winifred Jane Bloemfontein Clarke, was born on 29 March 1900 at No 4 Borwick Rails, Millom. *Author*

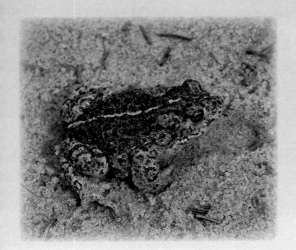

TRAVEL IN 1910

Coniston steam motor train, Furness Railway

'The croaking of a colony of natterjack toads did little to induce a good night's sleep.' *Peter Smith*

At Foxfield 'Tein' would probably have boarded the blue and white carriages of a railmotor and trailer designed by Pettigrew, seen here in a painting by C. Hamilton Ellis. *Bob Gregson railway archive*

enjoyed simple pleasures. They played card games in the evening and went to bed by candlelight, half scared by the long flickering shadows that danced up and down the walls. Throughout the night the rasping calls of corncrakes and the croaking of a colony of natterjack toads from fields opposite Borwick Rails did little to induce a good night's sleep!

'Tein' often told me of the awesome sailing clippers lined up against the harbour wharf at Millom, waiting to be loaded with iron before sailing into the sunset over the Duddon estuary, and what could be nicer than that?

The steam locomotives on the Furness Railway, in their Indian-red livery, must have looked impressive steaming into Millom station, coupled to the distinctive blue and cream carriages. For my great-grandparents and family, the highlight of the year was a day out from Millom to Coniston, during the Easter holiday. A steam railmotor was introduced to the Coniston branch in 1905, having been transferred from the Lakeside branch where

it had not been a great success.

If they were very good a surprise outing to the Victorian seaside resort of Silecroft, just 4 miles by train from Millom, would have been embarked upon to keep them going until next summer – simple pleasures of long ago!

I conclude with a few poetic words as a tribute to my 'old nan':

In a little town called Millom
fringed by the Cumbrian coast
our nan lived out her childhood
amongst the people she loved most.

The eldest of nine children,
her life there was never dull.
She was the one who cared for them
And troublewide her cup was full.

In the shadow of the ironworks
Nan's parents and family dwelt
Doing their best to make a living,
But poverty made its presence felt.

Summer days were spent on the shore,
Enjoying the food mum had packed,
Splashing around in the friendly waves,
Nan making sure her brood was intact.

At fourteen she went into service
As a downstairs maid to the gentry;
The days were long and wearying
And the chores were hard and plenty.

When her grandchildren came along
Tales of the past she'd recall
To the young ones at her feet
Remembering the days when she was small.

Now she is but a memory,
The much loved head of our clan;
How our family loved to spoil her
For she was our ever-loving nan.

Joan Bowman (c1990)

A tale of a seaside landlady

Workers' holidays were originally governed by the textile industry, though nowadays the weaving sheds of Lancashire and Yorkshire are virtually consigned to history with hardly a single bobbin left turning. However, it was my personal experience that Wakes Weeks were about stereotyped seaside landladies and exploration of Lancashire and Cumberland with Runabout tickets covering the Fylde coast and the Furness area. July 1955 saw my family destined to spend a week at a seaside resort overlooking Morecambe Bay, where we combined our stay with a holiday Runabout ticket. In the interest of self-preservation the name of the resort will not be disclosed.

The holiday was felt to have begun as soon as the Stanier Class 5 steamed into the platform of our local station with its red-painted buffer beam to take us to our chosen seaside resort. As a boy I went alongside the engine and jumped when it suddenly let off steam, reverberating loudly within the confines of the Victorian station and reminiscent of a giant pressure cooker. I enjoyed the train ride but viewed the resort and the seaside landlady with a certain amount of trepidation. We duly arrived at the digs to be met by the proprietor, who attempted to put my mind at rest.

'Hello and welcome! I don't think we've met before have we?' Perhaps not, but thanks for the warning! The landlady then attempted to reassure us. 'I'm sure you will have a good time here. It's lovely here at this time of the year and there's so much to see and do!'

Really there was not a lot to do, apart from have a walk along the promenade in the rain, where there was not even an end-of-the-pier show. In sheer desperation we could feed the ducks in the municipal park with our greasy fish and chips, or how

'Discretion overtook the better part of valour and we remained silent for the rest of our visit, hoping for remission at the end for good behaviour!'
Cartoon by David Eaves

about building sandcastles on the muddy and shingle shore – all things considered sheer exultation. But better still there were opportunities to be liberated from both the digs and the resort using the Runabout ticket.

We were given a quick tour of the house and shown the bedroom, bathroom and dining room with the fetching sight of the three customary bottles of vinegar, brown sauce and tomato ketchup lined up neatly on the table. My father quipped, 'I hope you all have a good memory for faces as there's no mirror in the bathroom.'

Father was instructed by the landlady to take the dining room seat next to the window, having perceived that he had a good appetite and seeing him tucking into his bacon and eggs might attract a few more guests. It was at this point that I remember the peroxide blonde bringing herself to her full magisterial height to emphatically announce the house rules –disciplinary procedures to be observed at all times or else!

'The house is out of bounds to guests between 10am and 5pm. I lock the front door at 10.30, so coming in late is not allowed. Breakfast will be at half past eight.' By way of an afterthought she announced, 'Oh, by the way, will you need a bath? Just in case you do there will be a charge of one

pound and ten shillings for the hot water and bath towels. Oh, and would you like your eggs sunny-side up?'

I hadn't a clue what she was talking about but just agreed and nodded my head.

'Now, do you have any further questions?'

I thought of asking her if there was any time off for good behaviour, but discretion remained the better part of valour. I remained silent, for any transgression of the house rules was simply not an option and furthermore there would be no remission!

'Ah no further questions. Then in that case I'll bid you goodnight and don't forget to be down for breakfast no later than eight o'clock.'

After breakfast the big event was to take a dip in astonishingly cold water at the open-air baths. Having survived the outdoor swim we sampled the customary Lancashire gastronomic delight of fish and chips and later in the afternoon a bag of cockles. Feeling nauseous, I was taken on a bracing walk along the promenade where my cockles gained a return ticket into Morecambe Bay. My Mum sent a risqué colour postcard of a buxom woman in a compromising position to her friend with the cliché 'Wish you were here'. Thanks, but no thanks!

To make matters worse, while sailing my

model yacht in the lake I fell in and came out drenched, cold and uncomfortable. I was taken back to the digs only to be rebuked by the landlady, which was an even worse experience! We did escape to Blackpool at least once, where there were about 12 variety theatres during the 1950s offering star-studded entertainment with many great names of the past. There was even an end-of-the-pier show. Perhaps there was life beyond that resort after all, and thoughts of a possible escape route began to emerge. By the way, there are no prizes for guessing its name!

A ride with Lady Godiva and birds as well

I remember the journey along the Cumbrian coast by steam train with profound affection, not least for being taken by my ageing grandma Bowman to the ancestral home of Millom, but also for a certain 'Lady Godiva'. As luck would have it, the aforementioned lady happened to be antiquated yet classy 'Patriot' Class 4-6-0 No 45519 from Preston shed. The esteemed lady was powerful enough to haul a long train of about 12 coaches up the steep gradient from Ulverston to Lindal. Throughout the scenic ride around Morecambe Bay behind *Lady Godiva* I looked forward to walking and birdwatching alongside the Duddon estuary at Millom pier.

A highlight of the journey was Arnside, where the Ulverston & Lancaster Railway had built the 1,300-foot-long Kent Viaduct in 1857. More than half a century ago, enthusiastic and equipped with *The Observer's Book of Birds* I frantically attempted to identify for the first time in my life oystercatcher, heron, curlew, redshank and shelduck from the window of a Millom-bound train. I'll never forget that day when the small black and white pictures in my little pocket book came vividly to life. I got the bug for birdwatching and have been fascinated by nature ever since. While the

'Arnside was the birdwatcher's and trainspotter's paradise.' *Cartoon by David Eaves*

Kent Viaduct substantially changed the topography of the estuary, today little has changed and trains still trundle over its girders – but thank goodness for good field guides and optics!

For me this has always been a great classic journey that embraces a historic railway infrastructure in close harmony with the industrial archaeology of West Cumbria. It also runs through an area that is teeming with wildlife, and all viewable from the carriage window.

To this day the sequence of station names and the journey itself behind an interesting steam engine of one sort another is fondly remembered. I dubbed it the 'never never line' owing to the fact that with all those stations we never seemed to be getting any nearer to Millom. On arrival there for the first time in my young life we walked to No 4 Borwick Rails, in the shadow of Millom Iron Works, and the home of Uncle Barker and his old Mum, great-grandma Clarke.

Barker Clarke: his bark was worse than his bite

Barker Clarke was born at Millom, the cradle of the Industrial Revolution. I was later to discover that the retired miner's entertaining stories of a life time spent in Millom were liberally sprinkled with sharp humour and wit, and usually some surprises.

In a close-knit community like Millom, news travels fast. It was common knowledge that Barker and two fellow associates regularly walked 'around the rocks' (the seashore) most days. They also kept one another company while engrossed in conversation in the snug of the West Cumberland Hotel. Another favoured venue was the time-honoured seat in the market square next to Millom railway station. Matters of all sorts were debated at length and judgements handed down, the person or persons being discussed going about their daily lives in blissful ignorance of the 'rulings from the bench'. One day they had a matter of extreme gravity to cope with while awaiting a train for Bootle, where they intended to gather copious bags of mussels from the rock-pools on the foreshore. The porter had blown his whistle and allowed a train to depart without them. I am reliably informed that the reprimand that followed could have been much worse, and by normal standards was a term of endearment.

Uncle Barker once made a major expedition from the wilds of Cumberland to the Capital and was curious about the

Despite the razzmatazz and the many attractions of swinging Blackpool, Uncle Barker Clarke caught the first train home to Millom. *Bob Gregson railway archive*

crowds of people on London's streets, prompting the naïve question, 'Where are they all going?' After residing in Millom for what seemed like an eternity, he once travelled by train to Blackpool for a holiday and ascended the famous tower to admire the view. Awesome maybe, but on seeing the distinctive and familiar outline of Black Combe dominating the skyline, across Morecambe Bay, he became unsettled and no longer wanted to 'be beside the seaside'. So on day one of his brief sojourn he speedily purchased a single rail ticket home to Millom.

Barker Clarke was a respected gentleman who always had a tale to tell. He rarely left Millom, but on the occasion of a rare holiday with friends to Pontins Camp at Southport, towards the end of his life, he fell ill. Someone cried out, 'Quick, we need a doctor!' Barker, ever the wit, replied, 'Never mind a doctor – bring a bloody undertaker!' Sadly, Barker passed away, miles away from his beloved Lakeland home.

A tale of two Davids

By the early 1950s Millom Iron Works had acquired a large assortment of industrial steam and diesel locomotives and 30 miles of railway track to remove mineral products and waste.

One July day in about 1954 Barker Clarke took me walking and I asked him, 'Where are we going?' to which he snapped, 'Never you mind.' I soon discovered that a surprise was to unfold on reaching Millom Iron Works. Barker had arranged for us to be met by the kindly driver and fireman of a Barclay steam locomotive that was about to haul a trainload of molten ore from the ironworks to Hodbarrow. We were duly invited to join them on the footplate for the 2-mile ride. With a certain amount of trepidation, I climbed aboard and as the train eased away from the industrial scene of the ironworks' blast furnaces, the outlook changed to a landscape of green fields fringing the seashore. This was enriched by a cacophony of sound, from the soft exhaust and shrill whistle of the engine to the joyful song of the skylark and strident calls of curlews and drumming snipe. As the engine trundled along the rickety old single track it acquired an unnerving swaying motion. With increased momentum the train may even have reached 40 miles per hour – perish the thought, and take your last breath! Approaching Hodbarrow a family group gave us a friendly wave and as the driver eased off the throttle the air suddenly rang with the clamour of squealing flanges as he brought the train to a halt on the edge of the sea wall. Within a few minutes a shower of still red-hot liquid was flowing from the train, simultaneously prompting a volcano of skyward pyrotechnics. Thereafter a blanket of thick, clinging pink dust blotted out the immediate area of the sea wall, leaving me feeling overwhelmed by the whole experience.

Following recuperation I was shown the last of the isolated ore mines, which happened to be the usual haunt of a charming steam engine with a crane at the boiler end known locally as 'Snipey'. This unique and quite bizarre steam crane was busy at work lifting pit props into two old wooden railway trucks. Working in harmony with 'Snipey' was an equally archaic Avonside industrial steam locomotive navigating the weed-strewn tracks and complementing the industrial picture of a working mine. More than six decades later the whole experience of that day is recalled with a blend of nostalgia and affection for times past.

I revisited Hodbarrow mine just before it was scheduled to close on 31 March 1968. In effect it was by then a working museum, encapsulating the origins of Millom's industrial heritage and an anachronism in the mid-20th century that was soon to become a feature of Millom's industrial archaeology. I felt privileged to once again be in the company of Barker, who, as a former miner, was an integral part of Millom's social history. The site is now an RSPB nature reserve bisected by the inner barrier or sea wall, which remains broken in places. The outer barrier, where the trainload of slag was used to strengthen the sea wall, commands good views of the

As a young boy I was to board the footplate of this Barclay saddle tank, Works No 12452333 for an unforgettable trip from Millom ironworks to the Hodbarrow mine with Barker Clarke. This photograph was taken in 1968, my experience on the footplate having been some 14 years earlier. *David Hindle*

'Snipey' the unique steam crane. *David Eaves*

Duddon estuary, and an RSPB public hide is situated close by.

The Andrew Barclay & Sons locomotive I rode on from the ironworks to Hodbarrow had been delivered new to Millom Iron Works in January 1953. It outlived the closure of the works in September 1968 and was retained for two years in the service of the receivers. After being sold privately it has been preserved on the Lakeside & Haverthwaite Railway and, coincidentally, has been named *David*.

'She knows, y'know'

In the 1960s there were long queues outside the Blackpool Grand Theatre for the summer farce starring Hylda Baker and Cynthia, her mute sidekick. What is not generally known is that the famous music hall double act are dubiously reported to have made guest appearances on the Furness line. Although there is probably no truth in the rumour, there was certainly a lookalike twosome that haunted Silverdale station's waiting room.

During the 'Swinging Sixties' we regularly went by train with our Runabout ticket for a day's birdwatching at Leighton Moss. In the depths of winter we then had to wait in the freezing waiting room at Silverdale station for more than two

1953-built Barclay 0-4-0ST *David* shunts wagons while engaged on duties for the receivers against a background of redundant blast furnaces at the closed Millom ironworks in 1968. *Both David Hindle*

hours for the 6.30pm Sunday evening train (usually hauled by a Fairburn tank engine working the Barrow to Preston service) to take us back to Preston. In those days Silverdale had a genial station master, Charlie, who occasionally lit the gas lighting in the waiting room and, if we were very lucky, made us a coal fire. Here a minute or two could be enjoyed by

the fire in relative silence while reflecting on the day until the peace was suddenly shattered by a visitation.

In the glowing and eerie twilight a tall elegant lady, sporting a brimmed hat, and her tiny Mum, who hailed from Moses Gate at Bolton, entered the room and instantly held court. From this strategic position in the darkened waiting room it seemed they had been watching the world go by since time immemorial. As mentioned, they bore an uncanny resemblance to the illustrious Hylda Baker and Cynthia of television and music hall fame, but this was more than a mere apparition.

Characteristically, 'Cynthia' remained speechless while her Mum 'Hylda' did all

'Matters of all sorts were debated at length and judgements handed down, the person being discussed going about their daily lives in blissful ignorance.' *Cartoon by David Eaves*

the talking, much to the amusement of waiting passengers. Evidence suggests that she had a slight speech impediment – from time to time she paused to breathe! We listened patiently while musing over their armfuls of copious catkins and pussy willow and what seemed like almost the entire flora of Silverdale now destined for Moses Gate. I was reminded of the comic's catchphrases, 'She knows, y'know', and as for the 6.30pm train, 'Be soon, I said – be soon!'

Suddenly Charlie reappeared on the scene and simultaneously the whistle of the engine was heard distantly at unmanned crossings on the approach to Silverdale. As smoke engulfed the platform, an escape route beckoned. We boarded a compartment and began to admire the paintings of C. Hamilton Ellis designed to attract passengers and excursionists to visit places both local and far-flung. Suddenly and without warning Charlie ushered the two ladies into the same compartment – there was to be no escape from the non-corridor stock. Charlie glanced at his watch and sounded his whistle at 6.30 precisely and there followed yet more frivolous questions and stories all the way to Preston, bless them. One classic question that springs to mind – Q: Where do you find little bustards in Europe? A: Usually on doorsteps, madam!

A double whammy at St Bees Head

The village of St Bees is served by an original Furness Railway station. Nearby, St Bees Head is the only stretch of towering precipitous cliffs on the coastline of England between Llandudno's Great Orme and southern Scotland. The distinctive red sandstone cliffs form one of the most dramatic coastal features of North West England, and are home to vast colonies of seabirds.

A visit by train to St Bees featured on one very hot day in June 1958. Accompanied by a friend, we duly arrived at the beach and began watching a grey wagtail close to St Bees south headland.

We were young and inexperienced birders and, thinking we had discovered a species new to science, we pursued this puzzling bird round the bottom of the cliff while watching razorbills and fulmars high above us. It was our endeavour to reach Fleswick Beach, sheltering between the north and south headlands, but with hindsight this transpired to be a very serious mistake!

It soon became obvious that a tidal surge was roaring in beneath the boulders strewn around the bottom of the cliff. We began to take some solace in considering whether there was perhaps life after death, though

The grey wagtail in more familiar territory. *Peter Smith*

We reached the top of the cliff amidst a sea of pink thrift. *Peter Smith*

not a plausible option. However, come hell or high water, without climbing irons, crampons and ropes we reached the top of the cliff.

So began a long period of reflection and post-trauma shock in the heat of that afternoon before we reached the isolated Fleswick Beach and an inviting azure sea. A spell of skinny-dipping was next on the agenda, only to be met by a large black fin

looming out of the water. I immediately adopted my Olympic swimming mode and safely reached the pebble beach; although we didn't know it at the time, the final diagnosis confirmed the fin to be a completely harmless basking shark. I concluded that a guardian angel must have been witnessing the unfolding events of that day, but more importantly we survived to tell the tale.

A sailing on the SS *Viking*

The port serving the Furness peninsula in the embryonic days of Lakeland tourism was Fleetwood. During the summer months through bookings were available between Barrow, Fleetwood and Douglas, Isle of Man, by the paddle steamers *Lady Evelyn* or *Lady Moyra*. The day excursion left Barrow's Ramsden Dock on weekdays at

Turbine Steamer "Viking"

9.00am and returned to Barrow at 9.45pm. At Fleetwood the paddle steamers connected with the steamers of the Isle of Man Steam Packet Company. One of the ships that regularly operated the service to the Isle of Man was the SS *Viking*, an elegant twin-funnel turbine steam ship that was actually in service before the *Titanic*, having been launched in 1905.

As was the custom during the Wakes Weeks of the early 1950s, large numbers of passengers made the crossing on the Isle of Man Steam Packet ferry. I was one of those not-so-old sea-dogs who boarded the SS *Viking*, and to rekindle interest in the area's nautical past I recall a voyage we made to the Isle of Man during July 1952.

NEW TURBINE STEAMER "VIKING"

Two images of the Isle of Man Steam Packet Company's ferry the SS *Viking*. *Bob Gregson railway archive*

My grandfather Hindle informed me, 'Reet, David, we're going t' island tomorrow and you're coming with us if you're a good 'un.'

This was intended to be a surprise, but with hindsight I wish I been a bad 'un! The following morning we duly boarded the SS *Viking* and on arriving at Douglas we enjoyed four hours on the island, but looking out to sea from Douglas Head it became increasingly obvious that the sea was rough and a storm was not far away.

The return crossing on the old *Viking* was traumatic. We had to endure a force 10 gale, and Grandpa stating that we should 'stay on deck and look for the silver-lining' was small consolation You must be joking.

'Best to stay on deck, son, and look for the silver lining.' *Cartoon by David Eaves*

It was cold and the silver lining was well hidden, the vessel rolled incessantly from side to side and the decks were awash with huge waves – Niagara sprang to mind! Somewhere at the lowest point of the vessel I lay on a bunk and just longed to shuffle off this mortal coil. Although I lived to recall the event, I vowed I would never go on a ship again!

The SS *Viking* finished her Steam Packet service on the Fleetwood schedule on 14 August 1954. Two days later she sailed for Barrow under her own steam to 'finish with engines' and be broken up. During her 49 years of service she must have carried millions of happy holidaymakers before being scrapped by Wards at Barrow-in-Furness in 1954. She was the last coal-burning steamer in the Steam Packet fleet. Prior to scrapping I caught a final glimpse of her distinctive twin funnels from the carriage window of a train rounding the bend at Salthouse Junction on the approach to Barrow-in-Furness station.

Camping coaches

During the 1930s a new era of 'hi-de-hi' holiday camps dawned, often served by train, together with railway camping coaches. This was before the era of mass car travel, when there was popular enthusiasm for outdoor holidays. Camping coaches were offered as accommodation for holidaymakers in rural or coastal areas with a convenient railway station facility. The old passenger carriages were no longer suitable for use in trains, and were converted to provide basic sleeping and living accommodation at attractive static locations. Sites along the Furness line included Grange-over-Sands, Coniston, Torver, Lakeside and Ravenglass stations, and at Bassenthwaite station on the Keswick line. The era of camping coaches declined from the mid-1960s as holidaying abroad became exceedingly popular.

During their heyday the charges for the use of camping coaches were designed to encourage people to travel by train to their destinations and make use of the local railway services. We spent a week in a camping coach at Ravenglass and used it as base for exploring the Lake District. The Pullman car *Elmira* was to be our home for a week; it still exists and can be booked for holidays at Ravenglass station. It was originally built to serve as an ambulance train during the First World War, with no doubt an illustrious history – if only carriage walls could talk!

Runabout tickets and Furness Railway branch lines

The 1950 and '60s were the heyday of the seaside landlady, camping coaches and trips by train with holiday Runabout tickets, a British Railways initiative that allowed unlimited travel with relatively few restrictions over a period of one week within a defined area. There were numerous regions available and my parents opted for area No 2 covering the holiday resorts of Lancashire and the Lake District, which included the Furness line. We usually visited the popular resorts, but at the top of the list for me was a journey along the Coniston branch, with the Lakeside branch a close second.

My holiday Runabout ticket serves as a reminder that No 2 area covered the holiday resorts of Lancashire and the Lake District, which included the Furness line.

At Preston we caught the twice-weekly (Tuesday and Thursday) excursion train from Blackpool direct to Coniston. Foxfield was the junction for the branch, where diminutive Ivatt 2-6-2 tank engine No 41217 regularly worked the local service between there and Coniston. The piercing hoot and exhaust beats of No 41217 and other labouring steam engines working the steeply graded line harmonised well with the wild and beautiful landscape. For almost a century local trains drifted along the valley between Foxfield and Coniston, passing the wayside stations of Broughton, Woodland and Torver. From Coniston station, high on a ledge above the village,

'Cheap family fun … the ten bob ticket!'
Cartoon by David Eaves

a panoramic vista unfolded of Coniston Water nestling in the valley below. Above, a certain Old Man of Coniston towered to 2,634 feet (803 metres) over the picturesque Swiss-chalet-style railway terminus. A stroll around the village and an aborted climb up Coniston Old Man followed. Later in the day we caught the bus to Windermere, which connected with a train via Kendal and Oxenholme to Preston.

A similar Furness branch line ran from Ulverston to Lakeside, Windermere. The branch was popularised by the working classes of Lancashire and Yorkshire, especially during the Wakes. As a family we travelled the line to Lakeside where we embarked on one of the motor vessels *Swift*, *Swan*, *Teal* or *Tern* for a cruise to Bowness and Ambleside. If the weather was good we did the journey up and down the lake twice, and all for no extra charge with 'the ticket'. A very acceptable alternative was to catch the Ribble bus from Ambleside to Rydal and walk over the bracken-covered 'red bank' to reach the pretty village of Grasmere.

Regrettably little remains of the Victorian Lakeside station, which was demolished following closure of the Lakeside branch on 6 September 1965. Freight continued as far as Haverthwaite until the line was shut completely on 2

Working the Coniston branch, Ivatt 2-6-2T No 41221 arrives at Woodland station in the 1950s. Note the period Austin car and the antiquated pedal cycle outside the signal box. *N. R. Knight, MLS collection*

A train arrives at the picturesque railway terminus of Coniston during the summer of 1947. *H. Bowtell, MLS collection*

April, 1967. The last British Railways train to travel the full length of the line was on 2 September 1967, when Stanier Class 5 No 45134 hauled a brake-van enthusiasts' special train. Thereafter the track was lifted between Plumpton Junction and Haverthwaite in June 1971, and Greenodd station and the nearby viaduct spanning the River Leven were demolished.

Since 2 May 1973 the northern section of the preserved Lakeside branch line has once again operated between Lakeside and Haverthwaite as a heritage railway. A fleet of interesting restored steam locomotives work the 3½-mile line, including two unique restored and working Fairburn 4MT tank engines, Nos 42073 and 42085, which significantly are the only remaining examples of the class in existence. Furthermore, this is now the last surviving segment of a Furness Railway branch line, and happily the historic link with the Windermere steamers at Lakeside has been sustained.

The former Foxfield to Coniston and Ulverston to Lakeside branch lines were interconnected with local industries and a pattern of rural life that led to the growth of the local tourist industry. All of the Lakeland branch lines could almost have been designed for pure enjoyment of the unspoilt countryside of the Lake District, but together with many branch lines nationwide they were felt to deserve no place the adventurous world of new technology that now exists. There is a sadness felt today acknowledging that life as many of us once knew it has changed radically. Set against such a background, the steam engine and the rural outposts that it once so faithfully served were inevitably faced with only one ultimate destiny – closure! For those of us who knew the traditional branch lines of Cumbria, they may have gone forever but will never be forgotten!

Ulverston to Lakeside: lament and renaissance

The accompanying photographs illustrate a chronology of railway activity on the Ulverston to Lakeside branch line before and after its closure on 6 September 1968. These were events that preceded its ultimate revival as a preserved heritage line from Haverthwaite to Lakeside on 2 May 1973.

Top and above: Three views of Fairburn tank No 42136 of Green Ayre shed, Lancaster, at Lakeside station on 1 September 1959. *All Peter Fitton*

Right: No 42136 passes the closed Haverthwaite station on the same day. *Peter Fitton*

Ivatt 2-6-0 No 46441 arrives at Plumpton Junction with the 12 noon Lakeside to Ulverston train on 3 September 1965. *Peter Fitton*

Class 5 4-6-0 No 44982, working tender first, climbs the gradient to Lakeside on that same September day, a scene that epitomises the era of the rural branch line, but not for much longer. *Peter Fitton*

The same train is seen in an idyllic location alongside the River Leven, three days before complete closure of the Lakeside branch. *Peter Fitton*

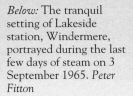

Right: The SLS/MLS tour arrives at the closed Lakeside station. *Peter Fitton*

Below: The tranquil setting of Lakeside station, Windermere, portrayed during the last few days of steam on 3 September 1965. *Peter Fitton*

Class 5 No 45134 heads the SLS/MLS tour of the Furness railways at Newby Bridge, the very last train over the Lakeside branch, on 2 September 1967. *Peter Fitton*

The start of the preservation era began with the transfer of locomotives from Carnforth (Steamtown) to Lakeside. *All David Eaves*

Above: On 2 May 1973 Fairburn tanks Nos 42073 and 42085 proudly double-head the special to mark the reopening of the Lakeside & Haverthwaite Railway. *Peter Fitton*

Left: Austerity 0-6-0ST *Cumbria* at Haverthwaite. *David Hindle*

Right: Fairburn tank No 42085 in Caledonian Railway livery nears Haverthwaite on 12 July 1978. *Peter Fitton*

6 Furness Railway locomotives and rolling stock

At the time of the First World War the Furness Railway Company owned 136 locomotives, 362 coaches, 3,939 open wagons and 2,335 mineral wagons, 304 covered wagons, 126 cattle trucks, 711 rail and timber trucks, 87 goods brake vans, and 357 service vehicles. The total length of track owned was in excess of 428 miles. The total of engine miles run during the year was 2,798,191, of which passenger traffic made up 837,664 miles and goods traffic 805 miles. During the first year after the end of the war 3,000,000 tons of goods and minerals were dealt with and more than 5,000,000 passengers were carried.

Until 1896 the Furness Railway had no locomotives of its own design. All were standard productions of the various makers, comprising seven types: 0-4-0, 0-6-0, 2-4-0 and 4-4-0 tender engines, and 0-4-0, 2-2-2 and 0-6-0 tanks. Once in office, Aslett appointed William Pettigrew as Locomotive, Carriage & Wagon Superintendent, serving from 1896 to 1917. As Secretary and General Manager, Aslett charged him with the task of designing and building more powerful locomotives, to the company's own designs, and improved coaching stock featuring corridors and electric lighting. It was unusual to see a Furness Railway locomotive in anything but a spotless condition, with the Indian-red livery always pleasing to the eye. It was said too that the carriages were luxurious and tastefully furnished, and worthy of special note were the splendid views of Furness scenery with which the carriages are decorated, and the electric installation. The last of the Furness Railway's locomotives were a series of five giant 4-6-4 'Baltic' tank engines, designed by the new Locomotive Superintendent, D. L. Rutherford, in 1920. These unique engines were arguably the most spectacular locomotive class seen on the Furness Railway; they stood 14 feet from rail to chimney top, the boiler barrel was 15 feet long, and the total weight 92 tons. The engines were numbered 115 to 119 and thereafter no more locomotives were designed or built for the Furness Railway before the 1923 Grouping.

In 1996 the venerable 0-4-0 *Coppernob* returned to the Furness area to mark the 150th anniversary of its first passenger service in 1846. In addition, the Furness Railway Trust is keeping the memory of the railway alive with its masterpiece, the 1863-built Furness Railway No 20, and an ex-Furness and North London Railway coach.

A gallery of Furness Railway locomotives

I am extremely grateful to David Eaves for his superb artistry and descriptions of the various classes of Furness Railway locomotives.

FR 0-4-0 No 5 *Coppernob*
Builder: Bury, Curtis & Kennedy, Liverpool
Date built: 1846
Wheel arrangement: 0-4-0 with tender
Driving wheel diameter: 4ft 9in
Cylinders: 14 x 24in
Wheelbase: 7ft 5in
Boiler pressure: 110psi
Tractive effort: 7617lb

Weight: 19t 10cwt
Date withdrawn: 1900
Present status: Preserved at the National Railway Museum, York

Coppernob was part of a second batch of locomotives delivered to the Furness Railway by Bury, Curtis & Kennedy of Liverpool in 1846, Nos 1 and 2 having been delivered two years before, and worked main-line services for more than six years. After use as a shunter around Barrow dockyard, the locomotive was withdrawn in 1900 and enclosed in a glass case at Barrow Central station until May 1941 when a German bomb wrecked the station and damaged the case. *Coppernob* can now been seen at the National Railway Museum at York, still bearing the scars of its wartime escapade.

FR 0-4-0 No 20
Builder: Sharp Stewart & Co, Manchester
Date built: 1863
Wheel arrangement: 0-4-0 with tender
Driving wheel diameter: 4ft 9in
Cylinders: 15½ x 24in
Wheelbase: 7ft 9in
Boiler pressure: 120psi
Tractive effort: 10,317lb
Weight: 24t 18cwt
Date withdrawn: 1870
Present status: Preserved by the Furness Railway Trust and exhibited at the National Railway Museum, Shildon

No 20 is considered to be the oldest working standard-gauge steam locomotive in the United Kingdom and was one of a batch of 0-4-0 tender locomotives supplied by Sharp Stewart & Co of Manchester between 1863 and 1866. Following just seven years of service, No 20 was sold to Barrow Haematite Steel Co and rebuilt as an 0-4-0 saddle tank. Upon withdrawal in 1960 the engine was presented to a local school for static preservation, and in 1996 underwent a complete rebuild including the construction of a new boiler and tender by the Furness Railway Trust. Resplendent

in Furness Railway Indian-red livery, the locomotive emerged two years later just before Christmas. After several years at the Lakeside & Haverthwaite Railway, No 20 has moved around the country starring at several heritage railway open days and is presently at the NRM's Locomotion outpost at Shildon giving rides to delighted visitors.

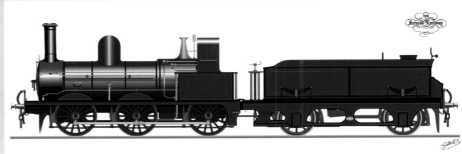

FR 0-4-0 No 25

Builder: Sharp Stewart & Co, Manchester
Date built: 1863
Wheel arrangement: 0-4-0 with tender
Driving wheel diameter: 4ft 9in
Cylinders: 15½ x 24in
Wheelbase: 7ft 9in
Boiler pressure: 120psi
Tractive effort: 10,317lb
Weight: 24t 18cwt
Date withdrawn: 1870
Present status: Preserved at West Coast Railways, Steamtown, Carnforth

Sold into private industry in 1870, No 25 is sister to No 20, and like No 20 upon withdrawal in 1960 it was presented to a local school for static preservation. In later years she became dilapidated and was therefore moved to Steamtown, where she awaits restoration. Our illustration shows No 25 in her rebuilt form as a saddle tank, although she would never have worn Furness Railway Indian-red livery in this guise.

FR 0-6-0 No 115

Builder: Sharp Stewart & Co, Manchester
Date built: 1881
Wheel arrangement: 0-6-0 with tender
Driving wheel diameter: 4ft 6½in
Cylinders: 16 x 24in
Wheelbase: 6ft 9in
Boiler pressure: 120psi
Tractive effort: 11,605lb
Weight: 30t 19cwt
Date withdrawn: 22 September 1892
Present status: Lost in the Lindal subsidence incident and lies buried 200 metres below the main line at Lindal

This was a very versatile class of locomotive used by the Furness Railway on both its passenger and freight services. Modernised in 1896 with vacuum brakes and steam heating, the majority of the class lasted well past 1923 and were taken into LMS ownership. Sadly, this was not to be the case with No 115, which ended its days at the bottom of a mineshaft following the infamous subsidence incident in 1892 at Lindal.

FR 0-6-0 No 27
Builder: North British Locomotive Co Ltd, Glasgow
Date built: 1914
Wheel arrangement: 0-6-0 with tender
Driving wheel diameter: 4ft 7½in
Cylinders: 18 x 26in
Wheelbase: 7ft 9in
Boiler pressure: 170psi
Tractive effort: 21,938lb
Weight: 44t 17cwt
Date withdrawn: 1932 as LMS No 12498 and scrapped

Classed as a 'D5', this was the 'go anywhere, do anything' locomotive of the Furness Railway and the final phase of the company's 0-6-0 type. They lasted more than 10 years after being taken into LMS stock in 1923, and proved to be capable workhorses around the Barrow area.

FR 0-6-2T No 93
Builder: Kitson & Co Ltd, Leeds
Date built: 1914
Wheel arrangement: 0-6-2 tank
Driving wheel diameter: 4ft 7½in
Cylinders: 18 x 26in
Wheelbase: 7ft 5in
Boiler pressure: 170psi
Tractive effort: 21,933lb
Weight: 56t 18cwt
Date withdrawn: 1929 as LMS No 11644 and scrapped

Built in 1912 by Kitson & Co, based at Hunslet in Leeds, this 0-6-2 tank locomotive was a development of an earlier design used in the northern reaches of the Furness Railway in the Moor Row area near Whitehaven. The steep gradients and tight curves demanded locomotives with a high tractive effort that were capable of pulling heavily loaded coal trains.

FR 4-4-0 No 132
Builder: North British Locomotive Co Ltd, Glasgow
Date built: 1914
Wheel arrangement: 4-4-0 with tender
Driving wheel diameter: 6ft 6in
Cylinders: 18 x 26in
Wheelbase: 7ft 3½in
Boiler pressure: 170psi
Tractive effort: 16,906
Weight: 47t 12cwt
Date withdrawn: 1932 as LMS No 10187 and scrapped

A very handsome locomotive, No 132 was generally kept on the lines east of Barrow on fast expresses to Carnforth, primarily due to its weight. The fine lines of its design have drawn comparisons to locomotives used by the London & South Western Railway. In 1917 two immaculate members of the class had the distinction of transporting King George V and Queen Mary on the occasion of a visit to Barrow shipbuilding works.

FR 4-6-4T No 115
Builder: Kitson & Co Ltd, Leeds
Date built: 1920
Wheel arrangement: 4-6-4 tank
Driving wheel diameter: 5ft 8in
Cylinders: 19½ x 26in
Wheelbase: 6ft 9in
Boiler pressure: 170psi
Tractive effort: 21,005lb
Weight: 92t 15cwt
Date withdrawn: 1935 as LMS No 11101 and scrapped

The largest and most effective locomotives produced for the Furness Railway, these handsome 4-6-4 tanks were affectionately known by loco crews as 'Jumbos'. The ten members of the class were the only inside-cylindered 'Baltics' to run in Britain and were used on passenger and fast mail trains between Barrow and Carnforth.

FR 0-4-0T Railmotor Mo 1
Builder: Furness Railway Works, Barrow-in-Furness
Date built: 1904
Wheel arrangement: 0-4-0 tank

Primarily used on the branch line between Foxfield and Coniston, the railmotor was the Furness Railway's attempt at reducing costs on its passenger services to some of its more remote outposts. The unit with its trailer could be driven from either end and proved a useful addition to the locomotive department.

7 20th-century developments

The opening years of the 20th century saw the outbreak of the Great War and, in August 1915, the shocking sinking of the huge Cunard passenger liner RMS *Lusitania* by a German submarine off the southern coast of Ireland; with the loss of 1,198 passengers. On Britain's Edwardian streets horse-drawn carriages gave way to petrol-driven motor cars, which were beginning to revolutionise transport. In urban and rural areas traction engines were superseding horses for agricultural use and the haulage of heavy materials. Barrow's electric trams ran hither and thither until finally reaching the end of the line on 5 April 1932, when bus substitution was a gradual process.

Changes of direction for the Furness Railway

Significantly, the Furness Railway was well-established by the early 20th century and enjoyed the glory years of tourism before the Grouping. It was the proud boast of the company that no serious accidents had occurred except the one on the Leven Viaduct in 1903.

Following the First World War Britain's railways were in need of new investment. The London Midland & Scottish Railway (LMS) was formed on 1 January 1923 under the Railways Act 1921, which required the grouping of more than 120 separate railways into the 'Big Four', of which the LMS was one. Locally, the companies becoming part of the LMS included the Furness Railway and the London & North Western Railway.

The LMS continued to operate the former Furness Railway network through to the nationalisation of the railways. It was the largest of the 'Big Four' railway companies, with routes in England, Northern Ireland, Scotland and Wales. Under the Transport Act 1947 the GWR, LNER, SR and LMS were nationalised on 1 January 1948, becoming part of the state-owned British Railways. Between 1948 and 1960 British Railways built 2,537 steam locomotives, but they were destined to lead short lives, some as little as five years against a design life of more than 30.

On 2 June 1953 Princess Elizabeth was crowned Queen Elizabeth II, to become our longest-serving monarch. An LMS 'Coronation' 'Pacific' locomotive bore the name *Coronation*, but commemorated the Coronation of King George VI and Queen Elizabeth in 1937. Another majestic member of the same class was named after the King. These and many other superb examples of the age of steam had charge of the West Coast Anglo-Scottish express trains, and although they rarely ventured on to Furness metals in BR days they could be seen on shed at Carnforth. Fortunately, two 'Duchess' and two 'Princess Royal' locomotives have been preserved for posterity: Nos 46229 *Duchess of Hamilton* and 46233 *Duchess of Sutherland*, and Nos 46201 and 46203, named *Princess Elizabeth* and *Princess Margaret Rose* respectively. These locomotives have worked steam excursions on the Furness line on several momentous occasions.

The twilight years of steam

During 1955 the British Railways Modernisation Plan was published, announcing the replacement of steam with diesel and electric traction. In the same year the construction of a futuristic prototype for British Railways was unveiled by English Electric as the world's most powerful diesel locomotive. It was built at the company's west works at Preston and named *Deltic*. The Napier engines provided the thrust and unique sound of this revolutionary locomotive. In 1961 the first production units entered service and took over main-line steam duties on the East Coast Main Line, making famous steam engines such as 'A3' Class *Flying Scotsman* and 'A4' Class *Mallard* redundant. Meanwhile the English Electric Type 4 diesel-electric locomotives (later Class 40) took over the top express trains on the West Coast Main Line and passenger and freight service on the Furness line.

The sudden introduction of prototype diesel locomotives to the Furness region and the first batch of diesel multiple units (DMUs) was ongoing during the early 1960s. This was to be the beginning of the end for steam on British Railways. The appropriately named 9F 2-10-0 No 92220 *Evening Star* was the last steam locomotive to be built by British Railways, in 1960.

On 27 March 1963 Dr Richard Beeching published his first report, *The Reshaping of British Railways* Part 1. But his plan to 'reshape' the railways led to the unprecedented contraction of the national railway network. The Doctor recommended that more than 2,300 stations be closed together with 5,000 miles of the 18,000 miles of track. This included all the stations between Barrow-in-Furness and Whitehaven.

Consequently during the 1960s vast inroads were made

These two 'Pacific' locomotives, Nos 46233 *Duchess of Sutherland* and 46201 *Princess Elizabeth*, have occasionally been seen working specials on the 'Cumbrian Coast' and 'Cumbrian Mountain' expresses. *David Eaves*

Top: The twilight of the steam era heralded the emergence of an 'Evening Star' – No 92220, photographed here at Keighley in 1976. *David Hindle*

Above: By contrast this 9F 2-10-0 on shed at Carnforth in 1968 was destined to have a one-way ticket to the scrapyard. *David Hindle*

into the massive fleet of the various classes of revered steam engines, of all shapes and sizes, both nationally and locally. At the beginning of 1968 there were still approximately 350 steam engines at work in North West England, but a rapid succession of withdrawals led to the finale of steam in regular service, on 4 August 1968.

Inevitably this heralded the closure of the last three remaining engine sheds on the BR network, at Carnforth, Rose Grove and Lostock Hall, and the scrapping of the remaining steam locomotives. Carnforth shed sidings became a morgue for row upon row of locomotives with their chimneys draped by an ominous sack, analogous to a menacing shroud. Fortunately, at the 11th hour many engines were saved from the cutter's torch. Those that were given a reprieve at Carnforth included two 4MT 2-6-4 Fairburn tanks and a 2MT Ivatt 2-6-0, which were to gain single tickets to the Lakeside & Haverthwaite Railway. The Ivatt was no

Above: In 1968 two Fairburn tanks, Nos 42073 and 42085, are on shed at Carnforth destined for preservation on the Lakeside branch line. Alongside No 42085 is BR Standard Class 5 4-6-0 No 7502 which was bound for the Bluebell Railway. *David Hindle*

stranger to the line having regularly worked it in the halcyon days of the old-style branch line.

On the evening of Saturday 3 August 1968 the last two BR steam-hauled passenger service trains departed within quick succession of each other from separate platforms at Preston station. The penultimate service was hauled by Stanier Class 5 No 45212, and departed for Blackpool South at 20.50. The very last diagrammed train was hauled by No 45318, driven by Ernie Heyes, and left Preston for Liverpool at 21.25. The final journey behind BR steam (excluding the Vale of Rheidol narrow-gauge steam railway in Wales) had taken only 33 minutes and 48 seconds. The following day, Sunday 4 August, saw the 'Farewell to Steam' specials, with six of them in Lancashire. This was certainly an historic and emotive weekend, with members of the public wanting to witness the end of an era.

Left: Preserved Ivatt No 46441, already resplendent in a new livery at Carnforth in 1968, was also destined for the Lakeside branch. Beyond is Class 'B1' No 61306, which had also been saved from the breaker's yard and subsequently repainted in LNER Apple Green and named *Mayflower*. In this guise it was a frequent visitor to the Cumbrian Coast line. *David Hindle*

A final Carnforth shed bash

The original Furness Motive Power Depot (MPD) had opened in 1882, closed in 1925 and was demolished in 1932. During the war the LMS's Carnforth MPD was built on the site of the old LNWR shed by Italian prisoners of war from Bela Camp near Milnthorpe. The new shed opened on 18 December 1944 with an allocation of 46 locomotives.

I visited Carnforth MPD towards the end of steam in 1968, when diesels were about to eclipse the remaining steam engines in service. It was a rapid and well-timed 'shed bash' to tick off the remaining examples of steam locomotives being prepared for the road. On a previous visit to an engine shed, Wigan Springs Branch, I had been unceremoniously thrown out by the shed master following a conversation that went a bit like this: 'Do you mind if we go round the shed, please? I've come all the way from Preston.'

To which he replied, 'I don't bloody care if you've come from Ashby-de-la-Zouch – you're not coming in my engine shed, so hop it'!

To reach Carnforth engine shed it was necessary to surreptitiously seek out a ginnel and gain a footbridge straddling the Furness line, with rows of mainly dead

A reminder of my trainspotting days: my Ian Allan trainspotting book. *Bob Gregson railway archive*

locomotives in the shed yard. As usual, I stealthily made a point of locating the shed foreman before he found and confronted me, and politely asked for permission to go round the shed. To my complete surprise, on this occasion, instead of being chased off, the nice kind boss granted me permission to enter the shed. Eureka!

I remembered Carnforth MPD shed, coded 10A, in its glory days, but by 1968 it was a surreal and rusting establishment that had seen better days. What a filthy, oily, dank yet fantastic place it was, with the predictable smouldering ashpit and

The monumental coal tower remains to this day at Carnforth as a relic of the age of steam. *David Eaves*

the sunlight casting shadows over the last of the locomotives in and out of steam on all six roads. Nearby the mighty coal tower and ash plant stood like sentinels over the last examples of steam locomotives as they slowly clanked along to a permanent halt, only to be branded with chalk on the buffers: 'To Crewe for scrap.' The distinctive sound of wheel flanges over the curves together with the sight of so many condemned locomotives struck a chord and evoked many memories. I was fortunate in being able to negotiate for a couple of quite unofficial footplate rides on a Stanier Class 5, have a conversation with the crew, and even have a sip of tea from the fireman's billycan.

Steamtown, also known as Carnforth

Carnforth was one of the last three MPDs in the country to close to steam in August 1968, closing completely in March 1969. However, like a phoenix rising from the ashes, Carnforth engine shed was reborn under the guise of 'Steamtown'.

My last visit to Carnforth MPD was inspired by a television newsreel clip featuring Dr Peter Beet being interviewed in the shed sidings. He gallantly stated, to the accompaniment of the music of Stravinsky's *Petrushka*, that if he could he would purchase the whole of the remaining fleet of BR steam at Carnforth. Thankfully his legacy was the preservation of several magnificent examples of British and continental steam locomotives, as well as Carnforth engine shed itself. Dr Beet formed Steamtown Railway Museum Ltd at Carnforth in 1965, intending it to be part of a preservation scheme with plans to restore the whole of the Ulverston to Lakeside branch line. Alas, this noble plan was not to be in its entirety, for the Lakeside branch line was severed at Haverthwaite due the development of the A590 trunk road to Barrow.

Nonetheless, throughout the next two decades Steamtown became a major regional visitor destination, attracting thousands of visitors and enthusiasts from Britain and abroad. Apart from seeing preserved engines and an operational engine shed, visitors were able to ride on a miniature steam railway. The site also remained as a major servicing point for preserved steam locomotives and associated rolling stock.

An open day at Steamtown featured the rare steaming of SNCF Chapelon 'Pacific' No 231.K.22 and the Deutsche Bundesbahn oil-fired '012' 'Pacific' No 012 104-6. *David Hindle*

In contrast to the giant French locomotive was this humble 0-4-0 Peckett saddle tank, named *Caliban*, seen here at Steamtown in August 1969. *David Hindle*

Class 5 4-6-0 No 44932 stands at Steamtown in August 1984. Also on shed was LNWR 2-4-0 No 790 *Hardwick*. *Robert Wilson*

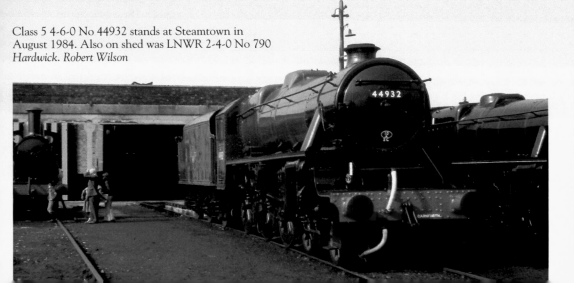

Diesels replace steam

The national and local railway scene was to change dramatically during the mid-20th century with the demise of steam, gradually succeeded by a new generation of much cleaner diesel locomotives and DMUs that started at the touch of a switch. By contrast steam locomotives required a lot of attention with more manpower and a great deal of preparation for the road.

During the 1950s the first generation of DMUs began to be introduced on the Cockermouth, Keswick and Penrith route, and gradually on the Cumbrian Coast Line. A pleasing feature was the panoramic forward-facing view from the front seat of the first compartment, providing passengers with a driver's-eye view of the many features of the Furness and Cumbrian Coast lines. This was often taken for granted and, with hindsight, I was sad to see the last of the traditional early classes of diesel multiple units after three decades of work on the Cumbrian Coast. They have earned their place in the history of Lakeland's railways.

They were replaced by the Class 153 and 156 'Super Sprinters' and the dreadful Class 142 'Pacers'. The latter tended to hobble along the coast line and seemed inadequate, especially when ascending the westbound gradients at Lindal; they were noisy and uncomfortable and, with the sound of gear changes and the wheels pounding out a recurring clickety-click, the class became likened to buses on rails.

Dieselisation brought a progressive range of diesel locomotives, with the first batch of 20 Metropolitan-Vickers Co-Bos allocated to Barrow shed in 1963. But they were only to succeed in setting fire to the shed due to technical faults. Consequently these newly introduced diesels suffered the indignity of being towed away by the steam locomotives they were meant to replace. For more than five decades an eclectic range of diesels has worked both passenger and freight trains from Class 40s to the very latest Class 68s.

Above: Class 150 No 150148 passes Plumpton Junction as an up local service on 25 April 1992. *Peter Fitton*

Left: On 4 September 1979 an old-style DMU crosses Eskmeals Viaduct forming a Carlisle to Preston service. *Peter Fitton*

Left and below left: The pioneering Type 4 (later Class 40) diesel-electrics were built by English Electric between 1958 and 1962 and regularly worked the Furness line. Two such examples are seen at Arnside in about 1980. *Robert Wilson*

Below: A new Class 60 diesel, No 60070 *John Loudon Macadam*, heads a down Padiham to Maryport empties train at Plumpton Junction on 25 April 1962 *Peter Fitton*

An infrequent sight was Class 20 Nos 20168 and 20059 working in tandem while hauling the 12.48 Manchester Victoria to Barrow service train across the Leven Viaduct on 25 April 1992. *Peter Fitton*

Class 31 Nos 31126 and 31410 head the last 16.48 Manchester to Barrow loco-hauled train, passing Plumpton Junction on 25 August 1994. *Peter Fitton*

Above: Class 47 No 47125 hauls freight train 6A49 from Corkickle to Willesden at Grange on 6 June 1992. *Peter Fitton*

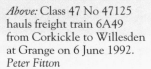

Right: This Class 50 was an unusual sight on the Furness line, and is seen at Plumpton Junction on an up Barrow to Euston train on 23 September 1972. *Peter Fitton*

8 A railway for pleasure: excursion traffic

Railway excursions are an important element of British leisure pursuits and railway history with their origins in the Victorian period. The Railway Regulation Act 1844 required all companies to provide at least one train a day consisting of 3rd Class covered accommodation, travelling at not less than 12 miles per hour, for which the rate was not to exceed 1d a mile. The underlying principle of the excursion train was that trains conveyed passengers to a variety of pre-determined venues and return with the benefits of travelling at reduced rates. Therefore many passengers took advantage of the reduced fares offered on excursion trains to and from stations on the Furness Railway.

In addition, higher wages provided fertile ground for the wealthier Victorian tourists and certain elements of the well-off working classes to enjoy the coming of the first railways. J. Walton, in *Lancashire: A Social History* (Manchester University Press, 1987, pp244, 284) argues that in Lancashire, 'Substantial increases in cotton workers' wages are not in evidence until after the Cotton Famine (1861-1864). The mid-Victorian period sees little gains in real wages, punctuated by severe economic crises and accompanied by persisting low standards of health and hygiene.'

Nevertheless, cheap excursions facilitated the movement of people all over the country, for the first time enabling mass travel beyond villages and towns. In 1867 the Furness & Midland Joint Railway and the LNWR gave birth to Morecambe as a holiday resort, and many holidaymakers travelled from West Yorkshire via Carnforth. The abundance of summer excursion traffic over the line from Leeds and Bradford in particular led to Morecambe being dubbed 'Bradford by the Sea'.

The growth of Lakeland tourism corresponded with the coming of the Furness Railway and the innovations of Alfred Aslett. A publication of 1916 (*English Lakeland: Furness Railway*) records the success of his commercial enterprise and his innovation in attracting Lancashire's holidaymakers to the Lake District with his combined excursions:

'Alfred Aslett had been serious in meeting the needs of tourists, and unrivalled facilities for travel exist, which add greatly to the pleasure of a visit paid to the Furness district. Weekly tickets are issued at about half the ordinary fare and weekly tickets, including cycle, allowing of an unlimited number of journeys between certain groups of stations, are issued at remarkable cheap rates. A magnificent series of tours through the Lake District have been arranged, tours which for beauty of scenery are unmatchable anywhere, particulars of which are to be found in the company's illustrated pamphlet "Tours through Lakeland". The carriages are luxurious, comparing very favourable with the carriages possessed by any other railway. They are tastefully furnished, and worthy of special note are the splendid views of Furness scenery, with which the carriages are decorated.

The great success attendant upon the Company's enterprise in opening out the service from Blackpool to the Lakes, via Fleetwood and Barrow, has been due to the excellent arrangements made, and the conveniences provided. The popularity of this service has been greatly enhanced since the acquisition of the PS Moyra, a fine steel-built vessel carrying 1,015 passengers, with a speed of 19 knots. This steamer in conjunction with the PS *Lady Evelyn* is admirably adapted for the development of the Furness Company's tourist business between the populous centres of Lancashire and the Lake District.

The needs of passengers at the various railway stations have received the careful attention of the company. The stations themselves are without equal for cleanliness and convenience, and travellers may rely upon every accommodation that forethought can devise. Although only some 74 miles in length from end to end, the Furness line has many branch lines, and a variety of scenery. From the stations on this line it is possible to visit all the most famous of the circle of Lakes around Grasmere and Helvellyn, which are comprehended in the celebrated Lake District.'

Notwithstanding the foregoing, regular train excursions became more accessible and the Furness Railway transported a discerning public from all walks of life to a small number of genteel Victorian seaside destinations along the Cumbrian coast. Excursion traffic was suspended during the

Above: During the Alfred Aslett era excursion passengers had the opportunity to board the SY *Gondola* for a cruise on Coniston. These two photographs illustrate how it would have looked in 1910, contrasted with its present-day appearance. *Courtesy of the National Trust*

Right: A typical advertisement dated 29 April 1964 advertising a DMU excursion train from Leeds to Barrow-in-Furness via the former Furness & Midland line. *Bob Gregson railway archive*

First World War by the Railway Executive, but post-war there was a renaissance in the number of day excursions, which peaked before the outbreak of the Second World War. For example, during the spring of 1939 the LMS ran evening excursions from Yorkshire, departing from Guiseley at 4.25pm and taking in the Lakeside branch to Windermere with the option of a sail from Lakeside to Bowness.

Following nationalisation in January 1948, British Railways was quick to

capitalise on day excursions, especially during Wakes Weeks. Throughout the 1950s and '60s rail excursions grew with the introduction of ramblers' and scenic tours to the Lake District. Special trains to football and rugby events were also popular, not least the Barrow versus Workington Rugby League Cup Final at Wembley in 1955, which attracted many fans. According to *Trains Illustrated*, British Railways ran 17 special trains to Wembley, hauled by an assortment of Stanier Class 5, 'Jubilees' and 'Patriot' locomotives.

The Cumbrian coast was popular with passengers, and the small town of Millom was probably approved as an excursion destination because of logistics: it had a turntable allowing steam locomotives to be turned for the return journey, and there were sidings for the carriage stock. British Railways advertised excursions in the local evening paper and the excursion train to Millom was only 5 shillings per adult for the return journey in the late 1950s. Stations along the line displayed colourful posters of the Lake District to encourage more tourists to the region.

Together with the Furness line, the former Cockermouth, Keswick & Penrith Railway (CK&P) featured in several excursions. The first Derby Lightweight diesel multiple units began to replace steam

special excursion

LANCASTER   ARNSIDE   GRANGE
ULVERSTON   DALTON   BARROW
MILLOM   RAVENGLASS   DALEGARTH‡
SEASCALE   SELLAFIELD   ST. BEES
WHITEHAVEN   WORKINGTON

Sunday 9th August 1964

‡Passengers change at Ravenglass and travel by Ravenglass and Eskdale Railway. Depart Ravenglass 2 40 pm arrive Dalegarth 3 25 pm. Return Dalegarth 5 25 p.m arrive Ravenglass 6 5 pm. Supplementary tickets to cover this journey at 4/6 adults, 2/3 children under 14 years may be purchased at stations

Children under 3 years of age, free ; 3 years and under 14, half-fare : (Fractions of a 1d. reckoned as a 1d.)

Tickets can be obtained in advance at Stations and Official Railway Agents

British Railways
LONDON MIDLAND REGION

BR 35000   July, 1964 P/153HD
T. Snape & Co. Ltd., Preston

We might have travelled on an excursion train such as this one, which originated from Colne on 9 August 1964, joining the train at Preston for Millom before the advent of the first DMUs. *Bob Gregson railway archive*

on the CK&P in 1955, with excursion trains running from Blackpool. 'The John Peel Land Cruise' used DMUs that ran during the July and August Wakes via Morecambe and the Cumberland coast non-stop to Keswick, where there was a stop of 3 hours before returning via Penrith and the West Coast Main Line.

In 1971 British Railways dropped the title 'excursion' from its nomenclature and introduced the renamed 'Merrymakers', a concept that continued under different guises, including mystery tours, which were popular in the 1970s and 1980s. These kept passengers guessing until almost reaching the ultimate destination, which occasionally featured Grange, Ravenglass and other resorts along the Cumbrian coast. By the late 1980s conventional rail excursions began to decline owing to a shortage of carriage stock and other logistical considerations, although steam excursions remained popular and still are.

There is little doubt that railway excursions enabled passengers to discover the English Lake District in the Victorian era and thereafter. Ever since the era of *Coppernob* the contrasting scenery of the coastal route, interwoven with picturesque villages and places of interest, has remained to be enjoyed by successive generations of passengers.

A memorable excursion over the Furness line and CK&PR

My initial encounter with these two fabulous branch lines was being taken by my grandparents on a special circular excursion to Ravenglass and Keswick on 29 July 1957. We travelled from Preston along the Furness line to Ravenglass for a round trip on the delightful Ravenglass & Eskdale Narrow Gauge Railway. I soon became aware that the journey up the tranquil valley of Eskdale was a real gem of a steam railway that would be difficult to surpass for spectacular mountain and coastal scenery. Back on the big steam train the excursion proceeded north to Workington.

Left: The excursion train arrives at Ravenglass station. *Ravenglass Railway Museum*

Above: At Ravenglass the delightful journey up the Eskdale valley in an open carriage behind *River Irt* was wonderful. *Ravenglass Railway Museum*

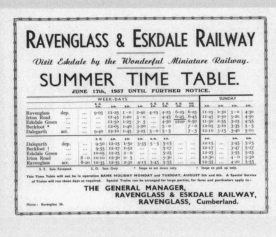

RAVENGLASS & ESKDALE RAILWAY

Visit Eskdale by the Wonderful Miniature Railway.

SUMMER TIME TABLE.

JUNE 17th, 1957 UNTIL FURTHER NOTICE.

		WEEK-DAYS								SUNDAY			
						S.E.	S.O.	S.S.	S.S.				
Ravenglass	dep.	...	9·05	11·25	1·0	2·40	4·25	4·25	6·25	11·25	2·30	3·0	4·30
Irton Road	...	...	11·45	1·20	3·0	...	4·45	6·45	11·45	2·50	3·20	4·50
Eskdale Green	...	...	11·50	1·25	3·5	...	4·50	STOP	6·45	11·50	2·55	3·25	4·55
Beckfoot *	...	...	12·05	1·40	3·20	...	5·0	...	7·0	12·05	3·10	3·35	5·5
Dalegarth	arr.	9·40	12·10	1·45	3·25	5·0	5·5	...	7·5	12·10	3·15	3·40	5·10
Dalegarth	dep.	...	9·50	12·15	1·50	3·35	5·5	5·15	...	12·15	...	3·45	5·15
Beckfoot †	...	...	9·55	12·17	1·52	...	5·17	...	12·17	...	3·47	5·17
Eskdale Green	...	...	10·05	12·25	2·0	...	5·25	...	12·25	...	3·55	5·25
Irton Road	...	8·0	10·10	12·30	2·5	...	5·30	...	12·30	...	4·0	5·30
Ravenglass	arr.	8·20	10·35	12·55	2·30	4·15	5·45	5·55	...	12·55	...	4·20	5·55

S. E. Sats. Excepted.　　　S.O. Sats Only　　　* Stops to set down only.　　　† Stops to pick up only.　　　‡ Stops to set down only.

This Time Table will not be in operation BANK HOLIDAY MONDAY and TUESDAY, AUGUST 5th and 6th.　A Special Service
of Trains will run these days as required.　Special Trains can be arranged for large parties, for fares and particulars apply to :—

THE GENERAL MANAGER,
RAVENGLASS & ESKDALE RAILWAY,
RAVENGLASS, Cumberland.

Phone : Ravenglass 26.

Left: A Summer 1957 timetable for 'The Ratty'. *Ravenglass Railway Museum*

Right: I was a passenger on this Grand Circular Tour to the Ravenglass & Eskdale Railway and Keswick on 29 July 1957. *Ravenglass Railway Museum*

Below: A general view of Ravenglass station in 1957. *Ravenglass Railway Museum*

2 RAVENGLASS STATION, RAVENGLASS AND ESKDALE RAILWAY

PLEASE RETAIN THIS HANDBILL FOR REFERENCE

RAVENGLASS AND ESKDALE RAILWAY

KESWICK, DERWENTWATER AND SKIDDAW

MANCHESTER ENGINEERS AND
LOCAL TOWN HOLIDAYS

An opportunity for the stay at home holidaymaker to have a splendid day out

GRAND CIRCULAR TOUR
TO
RAVENGLASS and KESWICK

MONDAY, 29th JULY, 1957

Outward via Grange-over-Sands

Return via Keswick embracing Morecambe Bay, West Cumberland Coast, Eskdale Valley and Cumberland Lakes

Allowing sufficient time at Ravenglass for a trip to Dalegarth by the narrow gauge railway.　Then proceeding to Keswick for a stay of approximately three hours

FOR DETAILS OF BOOKING STATIONS AND FARES
PLEASE SEE OVERLEAF

BRITISH RAILWAYS

E481/R.

At Workington the train was double-headed by two Ivatt 2MT 2-6-0s. These locomotives were specifically designed for light branch-line work. They took the train over the whole of the CK&P, owing to weight restrictions on the bridges to the west of Keswick and steep gradients east of Threlkeld.

Following a 3-hour break for a saunter round Keswick, the train returned to Preston via Penrith and the West Coast Main Line. It was a memorable day, the highlights being the line hugging the shore of Bassenthwaite Lake; the series of unusual cast-iron bowstring bridges spanning the River Greta between Keswick and Threlkeld; the quaint wayside stations; the gorgeous Lakeland scenery; and the crossing of Mosedale Viaduct nestling below the distinctive outline of Saddleback overshadowing Penruddock station.

The CK&P was originally conceived to supply West Cumberland's iron industry with good-quality coke from Durham. It was never part of the Furness Railway, having evolved independently as the Cockermouth, Keswick & Penrith company. The London & North Western Railway had running rights over the line from 1864 until it became part of the LMS at the time of the Grouping of the railways in 1923.

Keswick station is seen in about 1970 shortly before the truncated CK&P line from Penrith to Keswick closed in 1971. *Bob Gregson railway archive*

The scenic stretch of line between Workington and Keswick was closed by Dr Richard Beeching in April 1966. The section between Keswick and Penrith saw its last passenger train on 4 March 1972, by which time Dr Beeching was no longer in charge. What was once such a quintessential element of the English countryside has now been consigned to the annals of history. Today's heavy road traffic has superseded the railway and the steam-hauled 'Lakes Express', which used to run from London Euston to Windermere, Keswick and Workington – RIP Lakeland's lost branch lines!

9 An anthology of steam excursions on the Furness Line

There is something counter-intuitive about crossing spectacular viaducts spanning the tidal estuaries of Morecambe Bay and plunging into several tunnels along the route of the Furness line, especially behind a steam locomotive. This railway line harbours many surprises for enthusiastic passengers on excursion trains. It also has an uncompromising remoteness revealing contrasting seascapes and the unfolding panoramas of Coniston Old Man and Black Combe, and England's highest mountain, Scafell Pike.

During the 1970 and '80s I travelled on the 'Cumbrian Coast Express' behind preserved steam on several occasions between Carnforth and Ravenglass. Cherished preserved steam engines typically powered trains of 12 coaches and included LNER 'A3' 4-6-2 No 4472 *Flying Scotsman*, 'Coronation' 'Pacific' 4-6-2 No 46229 *Duchess of Hamilton* and many other memorable examples of steam.

In the 21st century, an age when steam locomotives have come to be considered as a creation of a more primitive era, it is like a breath of fresh air to see a steam locomotive winding its way round Morecambe Bay. Steam excursions along the Cumbrian Coast during the second half of the 20th and into the 21st century are a fine example of how the line is nowadays used for pleasure. The reborn steam specials and luxury trains of the 21st century with beautifully restored Pullman carriages have superseded the old excursion trains and are extremely popular.

Specialist chartered excursions organised by the Railway Correspondence & Travel Society (RCTS) and the Stephenson Locomotive Society (SLS) using preserved locomotives began to be publicised in the 1950s. Charter trains crammed with delighted enthusiasts became widespread, with trains often visiting the Furness region and Lakeland. The type of locomotives and carriages used depended on availability and the length of the train. The tours usually featured branch lines and used historic locomotives and, when possible, connected with the Furness line.

On 4 September 1960 the RCTS West Riding Branch ran an excursion along the Cumbrian Coast using an impressive array of steam. The tour featured the first visit of Midland Compound 4-4-0 No 1000 to northern England since its major restoration, and it hauled the train from Leeds to Carnforth via Wennington. Following arrival at Carnforth, 'Patriot' Class 4-6-0 No. 45503 *The Royal Leicestershire Regiment* took the train along the scenic Furness line to Workington. There was a break at Ravenglass for a return trip on the Ravenglass & Eskdale Railway, using the steam locomotives *River Esk and River Irt* and an unidentified diesel. Waiting in the wings at Workington were two delightfully twinned Ivatt 2MT 2-6-0s, Nos 46456 and 46442, and they took the train the full length of the highly scenic Cockermouth, Keswick & Penrith line. Finally, Midland Compound No 1000 hauled the train of nine coaches all the way from Penrith to Carlisle and via the Settle to Carlisle line to Leeds.

An attraction of excursion trains by steam was that they often used a variety of interesting locomotives, and visited industrial railways and occasionally closed routes that were not dominated by busy scheduled services. For example, on 27 August 1961 the SLS ran a tour of the Furness lines using Nos 43282, 44347 and 'Royal Scot' No 46152 *The King's Dragoon Guardsman*. The train comprised seven coaches including a cafeteria car. It visited the line from Plumpton Junction to the site of Ulverston's North Lonsdale Iron Works; industrial sidings at Dalton; the extensive Barrow Dock network; and the Hodbarrow branch line at Millom. It travelled the full length of the Coniston branch for one last nostalgic time, the branch having closed to passengers in 1958. During the tour there were 17 reversals, resulting in a very late arrival back at Morecambe. The itinerary is shown in the accompanying table.

Stephenson Locomotive Society/Manchester Locomotive Society 'Furness Rail Tour'	
Locos used: Nos 43282, 44347 and 46152 The King's Dragoon Guardsman	
Stock used: 7 carriages (BSO+SO+SO+Cafeteria Car+SO+SO+BSO)	
Route: 1Z44 throughout	

Loco(s)	Route
43282	Lancaster Castle-Carnforth-Grange-over-Sands-Plumpton Junction-North Lonsdale Crossing
43282 (2)	North Lonsdale Crossing-Plumpton Junction
44347 + 43282	Plumpton Junction-Ulverston-Dalton station
44347	Dalton station-Dalton Exchange Sidings
44347 (2)	Dalton Exchange Sidings-'end of single line' board near gate to Devon Quarry
44347	'end of single line' board near gate to Devon Quarry-Dalton Exchange Sidings
44347 (2)	Dalton Exchange Sidings-Dalton station
44347	Dalton station-Dalton Junction-Barrow-in-Furness
44347 (2)	Barrow-in-Furness-Ormsgill Junction
44347	Ormsgill Junction-Hindpool South-Loco Junction-Salthouse Junction-Parrock Hall Junction-Ramsden Dock South Side

4F 0-6-0 No 44347 stands at Barrow Shipyard. *Copyright Manchester Locomotive Society*

The 4F is seen again at Hodbarrow. *P. Moffatt, copyright Manchester Locomotive Society*

44347 (2)	Ramsden Dock South Side-(via embankment line dividing Ramsden and Cavendish Docks) Loco Junction
44347	Loco Junction (3)-Shipyard Junction-Dockyard Junction-(3) Ramsden Dock North Side
44347 (2)	Ramsden Dock North Side-Dockyard Junction-Shipyard Junction
44347	Shipyard Junction-Shipyard Station (Island Road)
44347	Shipyard Station (Island Road)-Shipyard Junction-Loco Junction-St Lukes Junction-Barrow-in-Furness-Ormsgill Junction-Park South Junction-Askam-Foxfield-Millom
44347	Millom-Hodbarrow Branch (end of BR lines)
44347 (2)	Hodbarrow Branch (end of BR lines)-Millom
44347	Millom-Foxfield
44347	Foxfield-Coniston
44347	Coniston-Foxfield-Askam-Park South Junction-Dalton Junction-Ulverston-Grange-over-Sands-Carnforth-Hest Bank-Bare Lane-Morecambe Promenade
46152	Morecambe Promenade-Preston-Manchester Victoria

On 13 June 1964 a major rail tour covering the lines of West Cumberland, commencing at Leeds, was organised by the West Riding Branch of the RCTS. The 'Solway Ranger' used historic locomotives, including the Scottish pre-Grouping Caledonian 4-2-2 No 123 and Great North of Scotland 4-4-0 No 49 *Gordon Highlander*.

Southern Railway 'Merchant Navy' Class 4-6-2 No 35012 *United States Lines* was the main-line power and took the train from Leeds to Penrith via Wennington to Carnforth. At Carnforth the train ran from the Furness & Midland Joint line briefly onto Furness metals before gaining the West Coast Main Line.

On reaching Penrith two Ivatt 2MT 4-6-0s, Nos 46426 and 46458, double-headed the train over the Cockermouth, Keswick & Penrith line to Workington.

At Workington Main three Derby twin-set DMUs took the train for a southward tour of West Cumberland's local Furness lines, via Corkickle Moor Row, Rowrah Junction, returning to Moor Row, thence along the closed line via Egremont to Sellafield. From Sellafield the train travelled north

along the extant Cumbrian Coast Line's single-track coastal route to Workington Main and through to Carlisle. At Carlisle the highlight of the tour for many passengers was to be hauled by CR No 123 and GNoSR No 49 *Gordon Highlander*. Resplendent in their pre-Grouping colours they took the train northwards and along the branch to Silloth, then back to Carlisle.

The outward journey took 45 minutes, and on returning to Carlisle No 35012 *United States Lines* was waiting to power the train back to

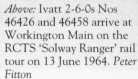

Above: Ivatt 2-6-0s Nos 46426 and 46458 arrive at Workington Main on the RCTS 'Solway Ranger' rail tour on 13 June 1964. *Peter Fitton*

Left: Class 5 No 45134 heads an SLS/MLS Furness rail tour on the Barrow avoiding line, leaving Park South, on 2 September 1967. *Peter Fitton*

The same train, comprising 11 brake vans, crosses Greenodd Viaduct with the very last train to Lakeside on 2 September 1967. *Peter Fitton*

Leeds. A nice evening ride along the Settle to Carlisle line was a fitting climax to one of the greatest and wide-ranging tours of the railways of Cumberland.

On 2 April 1966 it was the turn of the joint Stephenson Locomotive Society and Manchester Locomotive Society 'Lakes and Fells' tour, hauled from Manchester to Hellifield both ways by 'Jubilee' 6P 4-6-0 No 45596 *Bahamas*. On reaching Hellifield, LNER 'A3' 4-6-2 No 4472 *Flying Scotsman* powered the train to Penrith via the Settle and Carlisle line.

At Penrith the train was to have the distinction of being the last to be steam-hauled over the Cockermouth, Keswick & Penrith line before closure. Two Ivatt 2MT 2-6-0s, Nos 46458 and 46428, took the train all the way from Penrith to Arnside via the CK&P and Furness line. *Flying Scotsman* headed the train from Arnside to Hellifield, where Jubilee No 45596 *Bahamas* took it back to Manchester.

A remarkable brake-van tour took place on 2 September 1967, featuring Barrow Docks and Millom's Hodbarrow lines.

The tour featured the last train to traverse the closed Furness line from Plumpton Junction to Lakeside. Class 5 4-6-0 No 45134 powered the train from Carnforth to Barrow, where two Class 25 diesels took over for a tour of Barrow Docks and Hindpool Iron Works. Thereafter No 45134 regained the train from Barrow to Millom and Hodbarrow, returning via the Barrow avoiding line to Plumpton Junction to bid farewell to the Lakeside branch. The tour then traversed the truncated branches from Plumpton Junction to the Glaxo Smith Kline Works and from Arnside to Sandside before returning to Carnforth.

Following the withdrawal of steam from British Railways and the famous 'Fifteen Guinea Special' that ran over the Settle to Carlisle line on 11 August 1968, a complete steam ban on the railway network was implemented, lasting for four years. On the face of it the view expressed by senior BR management was that steam was finished and was not to be resurrected.

However, in 1972 steam trains returned to work excursions from Carnforth to Ravenglass and Sellafield. Approved steam routes emanating from Carnforth were to include the Furness and Cumbrian Coast line to Sellafield, and in later years through to Carlisle, and the Furness & Midland Joint line from Carnforth to Wennington.

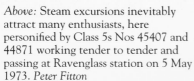

Above: Steam excursions inevitably attract many enthusiasts, here personified by Class 5s Nos 45407 and 44871 working tender to tender and passing at Ravenglass station on 5 May 1973. *Peter Fitton*

Top right: Class 'B1' No 1306 *Mayflower* and 'V2' No 4771 *Green Arrow* are seen at Ravenglass on 21 June 1975. This was one of the earliest rail tours and came from London Euston. It was a long train of 12 coaches, with two more added at Carnforth. *Peter Fitton*

Centre right: On 21 May 1973 *Mayflower* and *Green Arrow* made use of the now long-gone triangle at Vickers gun range to turn. *Peter Fitton*

Right: The same train approaches Seascale station en route to Carnforth. *Peter Fitton*

Above: Flyers like this were issued to passengers to promote the 'Cumbrian Coast Express'. *Author*

Throughout the 1970s and 1980s the Cumbrian Coast hosted the 'Cumbrian Coast Express', and here 4-6-2 No 34092 *City of Wells* leaves Workington with an up working on 4 September 1979. *Peter Fitton*

The route was extended via Hellifield to either Skipton, Leeds and York, or to Blackburn and Manchester Victoria to enable through workings.

What is believed to have been the first steam-hauled working of the 'Cumbrian Coast Express' from Euston to Ravenglass took place on 5 May 1973. Two Stanier Class 5 4-6-0s, Nos 44871 and 45407 working tender-to-tender, took over the excursion at Carnforth, thus overturning the ban on steam. One of the many highlights was the ascent, in each direction, of Lindal Bank, which behind steam, typically hauling a 12-coach train, was both

nostalgic and awe-inspiring. Arriving at Ravenglass there was an opportunity for a ride on the Ravenglass & Eskdale Railway.

The mid-1970s saw the operation of a regular summer service of steam excursions along the Cumbrian Coast Line. The 'Cumbrian Coast Express' started at Blackpool, picking up passengers at Preston, Lancaster and Carnforth, where steam took over from diesel for the run to Sellafield. Locomotives working the 'Cumbrian Coast Express' in the 1970 and 1980s included 4-6-2 No 35028 *Clan Line*, 4-6-2 No 34092 *City of Wells*, 4-6-0 No 850 *Lord Nelson*, 4-6-2 No 6201 *Princess Elizabeth*, 4-6-2 No 4498 *Sir Nigel* Gresley, and 4-6-2 No 4472 *Flying Scotsman*.

In 1974 Sir William McAlpine allowed his Apple Green LNER 'A3' 4-6-2 No 4472 *Flying Scotsman* to be based at Carnforth. Recalling the days of the regular 'Cumbrian Coast Express' in the late 1970s, for me the highlight was a journey from Carnforth to Ravenglass on 6 September 1979 behind *Flying Scotsman* and in particular the ascent of Lindal Bank behind the time-honoured old lady.

There have been several winter

excursions along the Cumbrian Coast. On 28 December 1982 *Flying Scotsman* ran a 'Santa Steam' charter to Sellafield. Other notable steam locomotives to gain Furness metals were the National Collection's preserved ex-LNWR 2-4-0 *Hardwick*. This veteran locomotive was overhauled in 1976 and hauled special shuttle excursion trains

between Carnforth and Grange in May of that year, and on the West Coast Main Line, one of which was double-headed with *Flying Scotsman*.

On 11 July 1978 the preserved 'A4' 4-6-2 No 4468 *Mallard* was given a rare opportunity to show that it was not an endangered species when it stretched its wings while hauling the 'Cumbrian Coast Express'. The excursion ran from Blackpool

Right: A charming photograph of old *Hardwick* crossing Arnside Viaduct en route to Grange while holidaymakers and fishermen seem quite oblivious of this historic moment captured on 23 May 1976. *Peter Fitton*

Left: Running tender-first, *Hardwick* is seen crossing Arnside Viaduct on the same day. The veteran locomotive actually attained a speed of 55 miles per hour running tender-first, though of course not on the viaduct. *Peter Fitton*

Right The famous 'A4' No 4468 *Mallard* returned to the Cumbrian Coast in 1988 and is seen here approaching the Furness & Midland Junction at Carnforth with a Grange to Leeds excursion in August of that year. The engine will go down in history as the holder of the world speed record for steam locomotives at 125.88mph (202.58km/h), achieved on 3 July 1938 on the slight downward grade of Stoke Bank, south of Grantham on the East Coast Main Line. *Peter Fitton*

and was steam-hauled from Carnforth to Ravenglass and return behind the famous escapee from the NRM.

On 5 May 1980 the Midland 4P Compound 4-4-0 No 1000 returned to the Cumbrian Coast to double-head with 'Jubilee' 4-6-0 No 5690 *Leander* on the 'Royal Wessex' excursion from Carnforth to Sellafield. The duo, resplendent in gleaming crimson, naturally turned quite a few heads as the excursion meandered around Morecambe Bay. The return journey was headed by Class 'V2' 2-6-2 No 4771 *Green Arrow*.

A 'Tornado' hit the Cumbrian Coast on 14 April 2010, and there were countless numbers of spectators to witness the event. Britain's newest steam locomotive, the Peppercorn 4-6-2 *Tornado*, headed an excursion along the full length of the Cumbrian Coast Line from Crewe via Carnforth to Carlisle, returning on the Settle to Carlisle line. *Tornado* has the distinction of being the first standard-gauge steam locomotive to be built in the United Kingdom since *Evening Star*.

More distinguished celebrities visiting the Cumbrian Coast have included the unique BR Standard 4-6-2 No 71000 *Duke of Gloucester* in February 2008, and a smart and gleaming No 46115 *Scots Guardsman*. The proud 'Royal Scot' was honoured by the Railway Touring Company to power a segment of the prestigious 'Great Britain VII' rail tour from Grange-over-Sands via Whitehaven to Edinburgh on 29 April 2014. In the 21st century steam nostalgia is perhaps exemplified by the return of the legendary *Flying Scotsman* to the Cumbrian Coast, with more exciting tours planned.

Above: 'Jubilee' No 5690 *Leander* is seen again hauling 'The Cumberland Sausage' towards Grange on 18 June 1983. *Peter Fitton*

There is little doubt that the excursion train (steam or otherwise) has added to the cultural life of the country both locally and nationally throughout two centuries of rail travel. Railway excursions enhanced people's lives by experiencing much that they wouldn't have had the chance to do otherwise. In line with the theme of this book, the Furness line has come to be regarded by many passengers as a railway for pleasure.

Left: A rare visit to the Furness line by the National Railway Museum's preserved Midland Compound 4-4-0 No 1000 was made on 5 May 1980. This delightful photograph shows it double-heading with Jubilee 4-6-0 No 5690 *Leander* at Grange while heading the 'Royal Wessex' excursion from Carnforth to Sellafield. *Peter Fitton*

The curious history of the 'La'al Ratty'

The Ravenglass & Eskdale Railway station is adjacent to the main-line facility at Ravenglass. The 'La'al Ratty', as the line is affectionately known, has become a feature of the landscape of the beautiful Eskdale valley, providing immense pleasure to countless hordes of people since the mid-Victorian era. The 'Ratty' owes its existence to the iron ore industry, centred near the existing terminus at Boot. In the early 1870s demand for local iron ore suddenly increased and Whitehaven Iron Mines turned to Eskdale, an area previously mined by the Romans. One of the challenges the company faced in this isolated area was how to get the ore from the mines to the Furness Railway at Ravenglass faster and more cheaply than by horse and cart.

The solution was obvious: In 1873 Parliament passed an Act to allow Whitehaven Iron Mines Ltd to construct a 7-mile railway from the Nab Gill mine at Boot in Eskdale to the station and harbour at Ravenglass. A standard-gauge track would have cost £90,000 (approximately £9,180,000 in 2016 terms), but laying rails to a narrow 3-foot gauge only cost £32,000 (approximately £3,264,000). Whitehaven Iron Mines Ltd and Ambrose Oliver, the contractor, took equal shares.

Fifty navvies started work in February 1874 and within a year ran trains to Eskdale Green. A steam locomotive, *Devon*, arrived from Manning Wardle in Leeds and the line opened fully for goods in May 1875. However, passing the Government Board of Trade inspection to carry the public took two attempts. The first passenger train left at 8.35am on Monday 20 November 1876, 'gaily decorated with flags'.

Unfortunately, the iron ore being extracted from the Eskdale mines was of such poor quality that prices fell rapidly and within six months of opening unpaid bills forced the railway into receivership. However, it continued to run for a further 32 years! Being the easiest way to transport goods up and down Eskdale, the railway carried produce from local grocers, coal merchants, millers and even basket-makers, although as a passenger route the local population sometimes joked that it was quicker to walk.

Eventually dwindling traffic and the poor state of repair of the line and rolling stock forced the railway to close in 1913.

An unexpected revival: the re-birth of the 'La'al Ratty' in 1915

When the Great War broke out in 1914 the old railway was overgrown but not forgotten, while elsewhere trains, tracks and complete railways were requisitioned for war service. The line's salvation came in the unlikely form of miniature railway engineer and model manufacturer W. J. Bassett-Lowke, whose new company, Narrow Gauge Railways Ltd, was seeking a location to test its 15-inch-gauge (381mm) locomotives.

This was a departure for Bassett-Lowke, who previously had produced model steam engines and ships as well as providing small trains for exhibitions, funfairs and rich men's estates, including the King of Siam (now Thailand). Narrow Gauge Railways Ltd purchased the railway in 1915 and gradually re-gauged the entire 7 miles from 3 feet to 15 inches, giving the railway its local nickname 'La'al Ratty', an old Cumbrian dialect term meaning 'narrow way'.

Originally the 3-foot track carried on beyond Beckfoot, up Beckfoot Bank, and along the fellside to the village of Boot to serve Nab Gill Mine and a number of quarries. However, Bassett-Lowke curved the track away from the fell, in front of the former miners' cottages, and over Whelan Beck to its present-day terminus at Dalegarth.

On 28 August 1915, only 12 days after a German submarine shelled the local coast, the first trains on the 15-inch-gauge railway ran as far as Muncaster Mill. Carrying more than 700 passengers in four days, the 'Ratty' was an immediate success. During the first year of operation it became so busy that more engines were needed to complement the only locomotive, *Sans Pareil*.

This locomotive, together with a set of open coaches, had been retrieved by Bassett-Lowke from Norway, where it had appeared at the 1914 Jubilee Exhibition. By the end of the war in 1918 *Sans Pareil* had been joined by another two scale engines, *Colossus* and *Sir Aubrey Brocklebank*. Unfortunately these 'model' locomotives proved to be lacking in power for the steep gradients and sharp curves of the railway. It even became something of a tradition for passengers to push the trains up the hills.

A further three locomotives, *Katie*, *Ella* and *Muriel*, were purchased together with wagons, coaches and track from the Duffield Bank and Eaton Hall railways after the death of their designer, Sir Arthur Heywood. The 1894-built Heywood locomotive *Muriel* was rebuilt and transformed into the present *River Irt* in 1927.

Meanwhile, the *Whitehaven News* of August 1926 reported on the refreshment room at Dalegarth station:

'Inside the refreshment room Mrs Wilson (manageress) and her staff had a tempting luncheon ready, the tables being adorned with sweet peas. The decoration of the room is in cream, picked out with a dainty shade of green, and the whole effect is charming. Wide verandas give shelter from rain and blazing sunshine, but are open to fresh air and the gorgeous views of Scafell, Harte Fell and the pastoral scenery of the valley.'

A new departure: the granite business

The 1920s saw another change of ownership, to local landowner and shipping magnate Sir Aubrey Brocklebank. Although predominantly a passenger railway by this time, a quarry had developed at Beckfoot and the railway carried granite from there to a purpose-built crushing plant at Murthwaite.

Passenger running was suspended during the Second World War, though the granite traffic continued, with services recommencing in 1946. Ownership of the 'La'al Ratty' passed to the Keswick Granite Company, which in 1949 hoped to supply the Sellafield site with aggregate for construction. Unfortunately, the presence of iron in the Eskdale granite made it unsuitable for use on a nuclear site. From Murthwaite to Ravenglass the track ran as dual gauge for a time, with standard-gauge track straddling the 15-inch-gauge rails. A diesel locomotive was obtained in 1929 to work this section. With the quarry becoming uneconomical to maintain, it and the Murthwaite crusher and the standard-gauge line to Ravenglass were closed and dismantled in 1953.

For sale by public auction

The railway now only carried passengers. With a short tourist season it was a liability that the Keswick Granite Co tried to sell. With no buyer immediately forthcoming, the railway went to auction at the end of the 1960 operating season. In the months before the auction, people came for a 'last ride' while a local movement was formed to save the railway for posterity. In early August Barrow railwaymen formed the Ravenglass & Eskdale Railway Preservation Society. Muncaster Parish Council held the funds being raised, though on the day of the sale it was felt that these would be insufficient to purchase the line outright. Fortunately two interested parties, Colin Gilbert, a Midlands stockbroker, and Sir Wavell Wakefield, a local businessman and land-owner, stepped in to make up the balance of the purchase price of £12,500 (approximately £262,600 in 2016 terms). The present-day Ravenglass & Eskdale Railway Company was formed, supported by the preservation society.

The Ratty's splendid steam and diesel locomotives

A new, larger loco, *River Esk*, was constructed by Davey-Paxman in 1923. It was to handle the heavy stone traffic, while being of sufficiently attractive appearance to look the part on passenger services. *River Esk* was designed by the famous model engineer Henry Greenly, who had also produced the Bassett-Lowke locomotives.

The scale engines *Sans Pareil*, *Colossus* and *Sir Aubrey Brocklebank* were built into the first *River Mite* in 1928, but unfortunately the locomotive was not very successful and was dismantled within a decade.

Despite construction of the 2-8-2 *River Esk* in 1923 and the rebuilding of *Muriel* into the 0-8-2 *River Irt* in 1927, the line was short of motive power. After taking over the line in 1960, the preservation society raised funds to build a third steam locomotive. The 2-8-2 *River Mite* entered service in 1967 and, although owned by the society, has been on permanent loan to the company ever since. Built by Clarkson's of York, the locomotive made history when it was delivered to Ravenglass by traction engine.

In the early 1970s it became apparent that, with passenger numbers rising, another locomotive was required. This time the company constructed the locomotive itself. The 2-6-2 locomotive *Northern Rock* was completed in time for the centenary celebrations in 1976. A further addition was made in 1980 when the company constructed the diesel locomotive *Lady Wakefield*. Other significant locomotives include *Bonnie Dundee*, built in 1900 as a 2-foot-gauge (610mm) tank locomotive before being donated to the R&ER by a member and converted to 15-inch gauge.

After a long career, including several decades running at Belle Vue Zoo in Manchester, *Synolda* was donated to the Ravenglass Railway Museum in 1978 and restored to the blue livery of Narrow Gauge Railways Ltd. *Synolda* is kept in operating condition and is an exhibit in the Ravenglass Railway Museum. *Shelagh of Eskdale*, a new 4-6-4 diesel, was built in 1969, incorporating parts from the Heywood loco *Ella* dating back to the 1880s.

Appropriately, three of the much-admired mainstay steam engines, resplendent in bright colours and in immaculate condition, are named after the local rivers Esk, Irt and Mite. The oldest locomotive is *River Irt*, parts of which date from 1894, while the newest is the diesel-hydraulic *Douglas Ferreira*, built in 2005 to honour the late Douglas Ferreira, who was General Manager between 1961 and 1994.

The train from Spain stays mainly on the plain

In December 2015 the Ravenglass & Eskdale Railway Preservation Society decided to purchase a new steam locomotive to bolster the railway's fleet. The international quest to find one had been under way for two years when eventually a second-hand steam locomotive was found in Malaro, near Barcelona, Spain. 'Pacific' locomotive No 8457 had been built by the German locomotive manufacturer Krauss of Munich in 1929 for the Ibero American Exposition, which ran in Seville until 1931. The Spanish Civil War had halted any plans for the creation of a permanent miniature railway.

The locomotive lay abandoned until a group of enthusiasts realised its importance and it was restored to a running condition. Unable to secure a site to run it, its future was uncertain until a team from the preservation society visited Spain in 2015 to consider its potential suitability for operating conditions on the 'Ratty'. Fortunately it matched the criteria for acceptance and the preservation society is currently undertaking a full restoration to get the locomotive back to running order.

Destination: the present day

The 'La'al Ratty' has been in operation for more than 140 years with new or redeveloped locomotives, rolling stock and stations. It is 7 miles (11.3km) long and runs between Ravenglass and Dalegarth stations in the Eskdale valley. Beyond

Ravenglass station the line is single track with passing loops at Miteside, Irton Road and Fisherground.

The railway uses the Radio Control Train Order signalling system and trains operate by radio communication between drivers and Ravenglass signal box. There are intermediate stations and halts at Muncaster Mill, Miteside, Murthwaite, Irton Road, Eskdale Green, Fisherground and Beckfoot. The railway is owned by a private company and supported by a preservation society.

Since the 1960s visitor numbers have increased to 120,000 passengers each year, with up to 16 trains daily in summer. On peak days in the summer months two trains depart from each end of the line per hour. The railway's capacity allows for a 20-minute-interval service. Trains run most of the year – the railway is only closed in January. The line is still known locally as the 'La'al Ratty' and its 3-foot-gauge (914mm) predecessor as the 'Owd Ratty'.

A portrait of the Ravenglass & Eskdale Railway

There now follows a unique gallery of historic photographs of the 'Owd Ratty' and the 'La'al Ratty' from its Victorian origins to the present day. I am very grateful to David Rounce and Peter Van Zeller of Ravenglass Railway Museum for their kind cooperation in making this pictorial chronology possible.

The 'Owd Ratty' was the subject of many picture postcards. The railway's second Manning Wardle locomotive, *Nab Gill*, stands at Boot. The station boasted a toilet (to the right of the loco chimney), though this was little more than a privy emptying directly into the stream below. *Ravenglass Railway Museum*

Left: Devon brings a train from Boot past the iron ore miners' encampment at Beckfoot. *Ravenglass Railway Museum*

Right: A crowded 1906 Bank Holiday train leaves Eskdale Green heading for Boot. On busy days the passenger stock was supplemented by wagons with benches borrowed from the local Parish Hall. *Ravenglass Railway Museum*

Left: The end of 'Owd Ratty' and the beginning of 'La'al Ratty'. The 15-inch-gauge *Sans Pareil* leaves Ravenglass in 1915 past the abandoned 3-foot-gauge rolling stock. The remains of the rear 3-foot vehicle, a locally built coach known as the 'Big Saloon', were subsequently restored for display in the Ravenglass Railway Museum. *Ravenglass Railway Museum*

Top right: August 1915 was the first season of 15-inch-gauge operation. The Bassett-Lowke locomotive *Sans Pareil* and a rake of coaches pause at Ravenglass. retrieved from the 1914 Jubilee Exhibition in Kristiana, Norway. They were completed and were complemented by additional coaches from the private Staughton Manor, Sand Hutton and Duffield Bank railways. The remains of the 3-foot-gauge siding can be seen on the right. *Ravenglass Railway Museum*

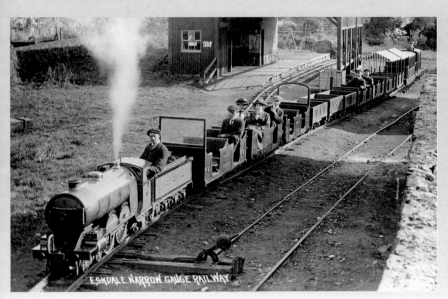

Left: Whit Weekend was traditionally a busy time for the railway, and 1921 was no exception. The Heywood locomotive *Muriel*, now transformed into *River Irt*, heads a train so busy that wagons have been hastily adapted into coaches. *Ravenglass Railway Museum*

Above: This 1922 view of *Colossus* and *Ella* at Ravenglass illustrates the difference in size between the Bassett-Lowke scale model locomotives and the larger, more practical Heywood engines. *Ravenglass Railway Museum*

Above: Sans Pareil and *Sir Aubrey Brocklebank* double-head a train at Irton Road in July 1925. Most busy trains were pulled by two locomotives as individually they were not powerful enough to cope with the load. It was not uncommon for passengers to assist trains on the gradients by pushing, or to pick heather while the locomotive stopped. *Ravenglass Railway Museum*

Quarryman, the first of three Muir Hill Fordson rail tractors, was delivered in 1926 and is seen here with wagons waiting to be loaded at Beckfoot Quarry in 1927. Today it forms part of the Ravenglass Railway Museum's collection. *Ravenglass Railway Museum*

The Refreshment Rooms at Dalegarth, seen in August 1928, were a popular attraction. *Ravenglass Railway Museum*

Right: The first *River Mite* was built in 1927 from the worn-out scale locomotives *Sans Pareil*, *Colossus* and *Sir Aubrey Brocklebank*, and is seen here leaving Eskdale Green for Dalegarth in 1933. The driver's high seating position gave him good visibility but left him exposed to the weather and liable to get a face full of soot, not to mention burnt knees. *Ravenglass Railway Museum*

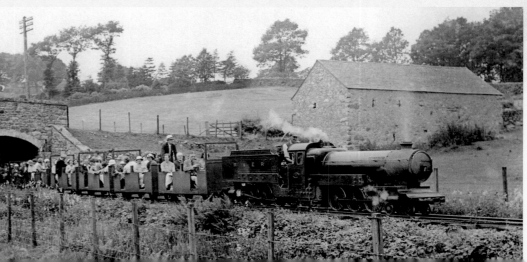

Top left: This is Beckfoot Quarry, a picture taken by the R&ER's Chief Engineer Tom Jones. *Ravenglass Railway Museum*

Left: The standard-gauge Kerr-Stuart diesel shunter is seen at the Murthwaite crushing plant circa 1950. The track under the lean-to canopy on the left is the main 15-inch-gauge running line. *Ravenglass Railway Museum*

Above: River Irt was rebuilt in 1927 from the 1894-built Heywood locomotive *Muriel.* It is the oldest working 15-inch-gauge locomotive in the world and works as hard in 2017 as it did on its arrival at Ravenglass in 1917. *Ravenglass Railway Museum*

Top left: River Irt and *Synolda* pass at Miteside. *Synolda* was built by Bassett-Lowke in 1912 for the Sand Hutton Railway near York, and is identical to *Sans Pareil*, the first 15-inch locomotive to operate at Ravenglass in 1915. *Synolda* remains in working order at the Ravenglass Railway Museum. *Ravenglass Railway Museum*

Left: River Esk passes Muncaster Mill circa 1960. The wide sleepers from the 'gauntleted' standard-gauge line to Murthwaite, lifted in 1953, are still in place. *Ravenglass Railway Museum*

Above: River Esk and a still-new *River Mite* cross at Irton Road on 15 July 1970 in the hands of R&ER stalwarts Benny Benstead, Martin Willey and Glyn Wells. *Ravenglass Railway Museum*

River Mite crosses Barrow Marsh on the Esk estuary in 1973. Scafell looms in the distance. *Ravenglass Railway Museum*

Left: Based on the typical outline of narrow-gauge British-built locomotives for export, *Northern Rock* was built in the R&ER workshops in 1976. The design proved so successful that two more, *Northern Rock II* and *Cumbria*, were commissioned for the Shuzenji Romney Railway in Japan. *Ravenglass Railway Museum*

Right: The Ravenglass & Eskdale Railway Preservation Society's diesel loco *Douglas Ferreira*, named after the General Manager of the 'Ratty' between 1961 and 1994, pauses at Fisherground station. Since the opening of the 'Owd Ratty' and into the early 21st century Fisherground has been a watering stop. *Ravenglass Railway Museum*

11 Discover Eskdale on the Ravenglass & Eskdale Railway

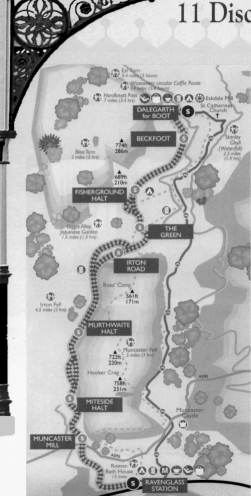

This detailed map of the route highlights the features of the Ravenglass & Eskdale Railway together with the principal stations, halts and facilities available at Ravenglass and Dalegarth stations. *Ravenglass Railway Museum*

A heron. *Geoff Carefoot*

Another way of enjoying the Cumbrian Coast Line is to take a ride on Lakeland's oldest heritage line from Ravenglass interchange station to the heart of the upper Eskdale valley. The 'La'al Ratty' also offers several possibilities for the ardent cyclist and hiker. A day out with a difference may be enjoyed by taking the bike in a converted carriage to Dalegarth at the foot of the Scafell range, then cycling back to Ravenglass via the beautiful Eskdale valley.

The terminus railway station at Dalegarth is the starting and finishing point of several walks in lovely Eskdale. Timetables, written guides to the railway and walks therefrom may be obtained by visiting the website. The wildlife that may be seen from the railway's slow-moving open carriages is described here to provide a taster of the ornithological potential of Eskdale.

The Lake District is rich in habitat diversity and the train ride itself embraces estuarine coastal marshes, tranquil woodlands, rocky crags, lowland pasture and gardens. After boarding the 'Ratty' at Ravenglass, several species of wildfowl and waders may be seen along the tidal section of the River Mite and the adjacent salt marsh. The open carriages are also likely to afford good views of cormorants and herons standing motionless in the shallow waters waiting for that tasty fish to pass by.

This colourful merganser can also sometimes be seen from the slow-moving

The red-breasted merganser. *Geoff Carefoot*

train on the tidal River Mite after it leaves Ravenglass. Fidgety redshank, curlew, oystercatcher and occasional passage migrants such as the greenshank may be observed on Barrow Marsh fringing the Mite, where flocks of greylag geese, shelduck and mallard are augmented in winter by wigeon and teal. Waders and wildfowl are quick to react to the outline of a peregrine falcon flying over, creating absolute pandemonium! The goosander prefers the upper freshwater reaches of the rivers and it is significant that the first confirmed breeding record in Cumbria occurred in 1950 on the River Esk.

Once the train has passed the picturesque Muncaster Mill Halt, the River Mite transforms into a freshwater river and closely parallels the railway. The line bisects woodlands and takes a course between Muncaster Fell and the river, where red

squirrels may still be seen at feeders, so look out for them. The national demise of the red squirrel is due to the northwards expansion of the grey squirrel, as well as other factors. Long may the declining population of red squirrels continue to be seen in Eskdale and throughout Lakeland.

Roe deer spend the day lurking in these woods, and creep out at dawn and dusk. Their crepuscular nature is often revealed by a sudden bark and a conspicuous white rear bobbing away up the side of Muncaster Fell. Any errant deer venturing onto the track is likely to be met with the shrill whistle of the steam train. There are fanciful stories that one can pick wild flowers from the 'Ratty', or so said my grandma, alluding to the 1920s! Nevertheless, in early summer blanket foxgloves abound on either side of the track, while the slopes of Muncaster Fell are ablaze with the crimson and pink tints of rhododendron.

As the train emerges from the woods the peaceful solitude is only likely to be interrupted by the soaring and mewing of buzzards rising on thermals over Muncaster Fell, and the bugle-like calls of the resident ravens busy mobbing them. Irton Road is 4¼ miles (6.8km) from Ravenglass, approximately halfway along the line, and has an original station building dating from 1875. In lineside gardens between Irton

Red squirrel. *Peter Smith*

Roe deer. *Peter Smith*

Road and the next station, Eskdale Green, insatiable nuthatch, great spotted woodpecker, greenfinch, chaffinch and goldfinch feed on a diet of sunflower hearts and peanuts, while blackbird, song thrush and the omnipresent tiny wren rummage in bushes and garden leaf foliage.

Steaming into the terminus at Dalegarth, the train crosses Whillan beck, complete with resident grey wagtail and dipper. At the end of the line there are views of England's highest mountains, towering above a pastoral landscape with cascading waterfalls and oak woodlands. It is hard to believe that Eskdale was ever anything but a pastoral backwater, but from medieval times it was a hive of industry with watermills alongside every river. Dalegarth station is an ideal starting point to discover and enjoy the scenery of mid-Eskdale. A visit to Boot is recommended to see the original terminus of the La'al Ratty' and to perhaps enjoy a pint in the village pub. After the nostalgic ride behind miniature steam, a visit to the pub at Dalegarth is, for me, the icing on the cake.

A great spotted woodpecker. *Peter Smith*

A chaffinch in the snow. *Peter Smith*

The goldfinch. *Peter Smith*

A dipper at the water's edge. *Peter Smith*

Buzzard in flight. *Geoff Carefoot*

12 The Furness and Cumbrian Coast Line of today

The Railways Act 1993 brought the privatisation of British Rail, which began in 1994. The ownership and operation of the nation's railways passed from Government control into private ownership and was completed by 1997.

These days, rail travel is considered to be more environmentally sensitive and a sustainable way of travel, while at the same time reducing traffic congestion to and from the Lake District. The principal service is currently operated by TransPennine between Barrow-in-Furness and Manchester Airport. This is supplemented by trains between Preston, Lancaster and Barrow as well as through services to Carlisle from Lancaster and Preston currently operated by Northern. The passenger

Left: Class 156 No 156448 enters Arnside station forming a Lancaster to Barrow local service on 4 July 2015. *David Eaves*

Below: A TransPennine Class 185 unit is about to cross the Leven Viaduct forming a Manchester Airport to Barrow service on 10 March 2014. *Mark Bartlett*

services are normally worked by DMUs, including Classes 150, 153, 156, 158 and 175, and Class 37 diesel-hauled trains, at least for the time being.

There remains a strong dependence on the line by the local workforce and commuters, with Sellafield station serving the nuclear plant there. Nowadays the level of freight generated between Carnforth and Workington is low, the nuclear flask trains to Sellafield being the principal traffic. This is a far cry from 1965 when the industrial scene along the line generated up to 80 per cent of freight traffic as opposed to passenger traffic.

The line was given community rail status in 2008 and has an active Community Rail Partnership

working hard to develop the route. It has a promising future with services operated by Arriva Rail North from 1 April 2016. Bigger trains with more space will provide additional capacity and have been provided by a partnership deal brokered by the Department for Transport and Northern Rail. At its inception Transport Secretary Patrick Mcloughlin MP stated:

'A quality rail service is vital to the local economy and tourism industry in Cumbria, which is why we have worked with Northern to bring these much-needed improvements to the region. As part of our long-term economic plan, we are transforming rail travel across the north by providing more seats, more services and better journeys for millions of passengers.'

There are different options for days out by rail over the Furness and Cumbrian Coast lines. These include the Rover Ticket, Cumbria Day Ranger, Round Robin and Cumbrian Coast Day Ranger, ideal if you want to explore the line in one day. Further details can be downloaded from the website www.northernrailway.co.uk.

Tractors on the line

Diesels operated by Direct Rail Services continue to haul nuclear flasks via Barrow to Sellafield, and certain diagrammed service trains are also hauled by the iconic Class 37 'Tractor' diesels. At the 11th hour passenger trains hauled by diesel locomotives have come back from the edge of annihilation in Lancashire and Cumbria; who would have thought that they would be resurrected in 2015 to work a regular passenger service? Nevertheless, in a remarkable turn of events diesels have returned to one of the UK's most scenic railways owing to a shortage of DMUs.

The Class 37 locomotives and refurbished Mark 2 carriages supplied by Direct Rail Services bear no similarity to the regular Northern stock. At the inception of the service the '37s' ran between Carlisle, Maryport, Workington, Whitehaven, Sellafield and Barrow-in-

Class 37 No 37423 *Spirit of the Lakes*, operated by Direct Rail Services, is about to leave Preston with the 10.04 service train to Barrow on Friday 13 June 2015. *David Eaves*

Furness, with four trains in each direction six days a week between Carlisle and Barrow. One daily morning train runs from Preston to Barrow via the Furness line. Currently the service uses two sets per day, with one spare at Carlisle Kingmoor. They are formed of DRS-owned Class 37/4s, DRS-owned Mark 2f coaches and a DRS-owned Mark 2 Driving Brake.

At the time of the introduction, Northern Rail Managing Director Alex Hynes said:

'The improvements along the Cumbrian Coast do mean changes to a number of services, and we appreciate it will take time to get used to them. However, the addition of the locomotive-hauled trains brings thousands more seats every day, improving journey experiences for our commuting customers and offering more space for visitors to this fantastic region throughout the summer.'

In September 2016 I took a ride on the 10.04 weekday service from Preston to Barrow, where I changed to reach my destination at Millom. To my surprise, prior to departure from Preston I was thrilled to see (and hear) a Class 37, characteristically growling loudly at the head of the train. The locomotive, No 37403 *Isle of Mull*, was in immaculate external condition, painted blue with an extra-large British Rail logo – the 'double arrow' symbol used extensively by British Rail, is still the generic sign for a railway station.

With tongue in cheek I spoke to the friendly driver, asking him if it was a special and if the locomotive had been brought out of a museum? He responded, 'No it's a service train and yes, it is on hire from a heritage railway in Scotland.'

I replied, 'I'll bet it is a long time since you drove one like this.'

He answered, 'Yes, it's 25 years since I drove one of these and they had to send us on a refresher course. We did have two 37s topping and tailing but we now have a driving trailer so we only need the one loco at the front of the train. My mate on the footplate is a trainee learning how to drive this 50-year-old lady.'

I boarded a comfortable Mark 2 carriage and within minutes the old locomotive went into a frenzied roar and eased off from Preston station for the scenic and enjoyable ride to Barrow-in-Furness. At Barrow I changed platforms for a train headed by yet another Class 37, to take me round the Duddon estuary to my destination, Millom. I had to adapt to slam doors and anticipate the train being too long for some of the station platforms, but this was not found to be a problem at Barrow or Millom.

The Cumbrian Coast route is one of the last regular diagrammed diesel-hauled passenger services in England. However, it has been reported in the railway press that Northern will stop using locomotive-hauled trains supplied by Direct Rail Services on 5 January 2019, so go for it now while the opportunity arises!

Class 37 No 37423 is seen again in the passing loop of the single-line section at St Bees station, passing a southbound service headed by a DRS-owned Mark 2 Driving Brake. *David Eaves*

West Coast Railways

Today the West Coast Railways Company Ltd operates an impressive railway repair and operating facility on the site of Carnforth MPD. It also runs private charter heritage steam and diesel trains across the UK national railway network. The former MPD itself has six standard-gauge tracks each with full-length inspection pits. The engine shed, ash and coal plants, the water tower, wagon repair workshop and vacuum-operated locomotive turntable supplied by Cowans Sheldon of Carlisle are all Grade II-listed. Remarkably the whole complex is a complete and unique example of a steam engine motive power depot. Unfortunately, in 1998, owing

to increasing Health and Safety Executive regulations affecting the site and the demands of supplying and servicing steam locomotives, a decision was taken not to reopen Carnforth as a museum or visitor attraction.

It is good to know that the Furness line has a promising future with increased services, upgraded stations and the provision of more diesel-hauled passenger trains for extra comfort. I sincerely hope that the railway's fortunes will prosper and that its enduring appeal will continue to serve and delight all passengers while under the franchise of Arriva Rail North.

Above right: Class 37 No 37402 *Stephen Middlemore 23.12.1954 - 8.6.2013* is seen here at Barrow-in-Furness waiting for passengers (including the author) to board for stations to Carlisle. It was built at English Electric's Vulcan Foundry and released to traffic on 4 April 1965 as No D6974. *David Eaves*

Right: A reminder of the Furness Railway of yesteryear: 8F No 48151 crosses the viaduct over the Kent estuary on 30 March 2002. *Peter Fitton*

13 Great birdwatching and heritage walks from stations along the Cumbrian coast

Nature reserves of international importance abound all along the Cumbrian Coast. Intermittently the railway hugs the shoreline linking the waters of Morecambe Bay with the Solway Firth, both Sites of Special Scientific Interest (SSSI) and given top European conservation status. Together with the Duddon estuary, they form part of the Natura 2000 network of internationally protected areas, with some of the largest concentrations of wildlife in the UK.

Passengers continue to use the wayside stations along the Cumbrian Coast and trains still stop at Millom, Ravenglass, Seascale, Sellafield and St Bees. There are also many request stops along the route. Typically people with rucksacks – just like me, in fact – alight at stations such as the request stop at Silecroft and disappear to ascend Black Combe or walk back to Millom across undisturbed golden sands.

Whether it is a relaxing stroll around Leighton Moss nature reserve or a more strenuous climb to the summit of Black Combe, there is something to enjoy for people of all ages and abilities – but always be in possession of either the latest technology or appropriate Ordnance Survey maps to aid navigation.

All of the following eight described walks are intended to be enjoyed by beginners and expert ornithologists alike. They have been carefully chosen to correspond with stations, thus providing greater freedom to complete linear and circular walks. Moreover, with a little planning, the walker can explore the Lake District by bus from stations along the Cumbrian coast (see the 'Augmented bus services' section below). Researching and undertaking these walks has been a stimulating and enjoyable experience to be shared with the reader.

The River Leven estuary is bisected by the railway viaduct at the point where it flows into the wide expanse of Morecambe Bay. *Neal Hardy*

Walk 1: Leighton Moss RSPB Nature Reserve

This circular walk starts and finishes at Silverdale station, which is only a short distance from the nature reserve.

Distance: Approximately 4 kilometres (full tour of hides)

Time: 5 hours

Grade: Easy to moderate

General: Refreshment, toilet and car parking facilities and a gift shop are available at Leighton Moss Visitor Centre and Silverdale railway station. The Visitor Centre issues permits, and news of the latest sightings may be obtained.

Directions: This walk embraces the whole of the reserve. From the Visitor Centre take the path alongside the main road towards Yealand Redmayne. Continue right along a board walk and take the right turn along the causeway across the centre of the reserve towards the public and lower hides. From the lower hide follow the path around the head of the valley and out onto the road. Turn left and eventually rejoin the path just past the causeway entrance, then either return to the visitor centre for a welcome coffee or follow the signs to Lilian's, Tim Jackson and Griesdale hides. For more variety, a visit to the two hides overlooking the shore pools is also recommended.

There is plenty to occupy a full day at Leighton Moss and there are many nice walks and much to discover close by. I have been visiting Leighton since September 1957, and one of the highlights of my birding career was finding a nightjar's nest with two beautiful marble-coloured eggs at nearby Warton Crag on 10 July 1960. Subsequently two young were ringed by my good friend John Wilson BEM, who was appointed warden when Leighton Moss first became a nature reserve in 1962, and served as senior warden at the reserve for 35 years. Sadly the breeding population of nightjars is long gone and the species is rare in Lancashire and Cumbria.

To this day two of the star attractions at Leighton are the rare bittern and the shy otter. They may be observed from the lookout tower or from all of the reserve's hides, although the Lower Pool hide is particularly good for sightings of the essentially crepuscular otter. When the moss is partially frozen is a good time to look for bitterns skulking around in the reed bed or making their occasional short, low flights.

Though detached from Leighton, the salt marsh is part of the reserve and is probably best reached by car. The Eric Morecambe and Allen Pool shore hides are good for wildfowl, gulls and waders.

Kingfisher. *Peter Smith*

Bearded tit. *Peter Smith*

Black-tailed godwit in flight. *Geoff Carefoot*

In winter the charismatic kingfisher occasionally makes a guest appearance on the fence alongside the marsh pools and large flocks of black tailed godwit are frequently seen.

Lilian's Hide gives excellent views over the mere and the extensive reed beds. It is usually the best hide to watch the breeding marsh harriers. Early in the spring they undertake spectacular aerial displays interspersed with bouts of nest-building. For much of the year this hide is the best place to witness the evening spectacular as thousands of starlings, swallows and sand martins come in to roost in the reed beds. The impressive starling murmuration

at Leighton Moss, with up to 100,000 in some years, begins in late October/early November, and is at its best in November and December. The flocks of starlings are mainly made up of migrant starlings from Scandinavia and Eastern Europe.

The Tim Jackson and Griesdale hides are good for seeing the surface-feeding ducks, especially teal, shoveler, gadwall and wigeon, and during the twilight hours red deer sometimes put in a guest appearance in the open areas of the reed bed. Large numbers of black-tailed godwit have been present in recent years, and lapwings and snipe are frequently observed.

Many visitors come to see the bittern, and the best time to see one is during winter when the moss is partially frozen.

Marsh Harrier. *Peter Smith*

The public bridleway across the moss is known as the causeway, and is a good place to search for the extremely secretive water rail, and the best place to look for bearded tits, another Leighton speciality. Bearded tits are most active in the morning and the first clue to their presence is the distinctive 'pinging' call. One feature you may notice as you walk down the causeway is the old stone gate posts; the most noticeable are by the causeway bridge and provide evidence of the area's former agricultural status as rich arable land. From 1840 to 1917 the Leighton valley was drained by a series of steam-driven pumps. It was known as the 'Golden Valley' because of the abundant crops, roots and cereal it produced.

The public hide overlooks the largest area of water on the reserve, known as the main pool. From the hide good views may be had of a range of wildfowl, which in winter may include the pochard, tufted duck, mallard, gadwall, teal, wigeon, pintail, goosander and goldeneye.

Scan the surrounding limestone hills and woods for soaring buzzards and passing ravens, as both have increased markedly in recent years. The path to the lower hides passes through willow woodland adjoining the fen, then limestone woodland. Both are excellent for the commoner woodland birds and summer visitors, especially warblers. Breeding birds here include sedge warblers and reed buntings together with the occasional grasshopper warbler. In winter mixed flocks of siskin, redpoll and goldfinch feed in the fringing alders. The lower hide provides good views of open water and a good assortment of wildfowl. The dead trees at the back of the mere are well used by grey herons and cormorants and occasionally by passing ospreys. Finally, from this hide don't forget to keep ceaseless watch for the elusive otter, and you may well be rewarded.

The garganey is an uncommon spring passage migrant and summer visitor to Leighton Moss, and with a bit of luck it may be spotted from any of the hides. *Geoff Carefoot*

Walk 2: The two Arnsides – a coastal circular walk via Far Arnside and Arnside Knott

This circular walk starts and finishes at Arnside railway station.

Distance: 9 kilometres.

Time: 5 hours

Grade: Easy to moderate

General: Refreshments, toilet and car parking facilities are available at Arnside.

Directions: From the station turn right onto the road to reach the promenade overlooking the Kent estuary and continue straight past the Albion public house onto a concrete footpath indicated as 'New Barns'. After passing the coastguard station, the path ends on the pebble beach before regaining a track leading past cottages at New Barns Bay and on to Blackstone Point and White Creek woodland caravan site. At the caravan site follow a footpath sign to Far Arnside, via the scenic cliff-top footpath and the limestone promontory of Park Point. Be aware that between White Creek and Far Arnside the footpath follows the edge of low limestone cliffs that are potentially dangerous and children should be closely supervised. Follow the footpath through woodlands and Holgate's caravan site to Far Arnside. Thereafter proceed along a minor lane to Hollin's Farm. Follow

a footpath left along the edge of a field with a wall on the right and continue following the signs to Arnside, via the summit of Arnside Knott. From the car park descend the lower slopes of the Knott along a tarmac road that joins Redhills Road. At the junction with Silverdale Road turn left then right into Chapel Lane and continue along a narrow footpath that eventually ends at the railway station.

The two Arnsides are well worth exploring both for wildlife and for the superb views of Morecambe Bay and Lakeland's mountains from Arnside Knott. It is recommended to commence the walk about 1½ hours before high water, preferably coinciding with the tidal spectacle of the 'Kent bore'. At Arnside a siren warns of the incoming tide. After witnessing the initial tidal surge or bore, which varies enormously in strength and speed, you will be amazed how quickly the tide submerges the bay's intertidal sand flats. Always keep off these areas unless accompanied by a qualified guide.

Arnside promenade provides an opportunity to observe the main Kent channel before its emergence into the bay. Take a walk down the pier west of the viaduct built by the railway company in order to compensate for the loss of trade further up river when ships could no longer reach Milnthorpe. The sand flats and channel of the River Kent have flocks of redshank, greenshank, oystercatcher, lapwing and curlew, mallard and shelduck, heron and cormorant. Scrutinising the waders may pay dividends, for less common examples including the little stint, curlew sandpiper and rare American vagrant waders have been seen here. Take a close look at gulls, for among five or six regular species there is a possibility of seeing the yellow-legged gull, an uncommon visitor from Mediterranean climes that has been recorded either side of the railway viaduct.

At the west end of the promenade, on a low cliff is a small clump of the rare but beautiful maidenhair fern. At New Barns take a look at the smaller birds rising from the marsh, which may include the meadow pipit, pied and grey wagtail and, in spring and autumn, the handsome wheatear. The cliff-top footpath between White Creek and Arnside Point affords an opportunity to birdwatch across the bay and perhaps even to indulge in luncheon!

Birds can be a bit thin on the ground in summer, but spring passage highlights have included Arctic skua, red-throated diver, short-eared owl and storm-driven sea birds. Winter wildfowl and wader flocks feature wigeon, teal, mallard, shelduck, goosander, red-breasted merganser, ringed plover, lapwing, curlew, knot, oystercatcher, dunlin and redshank. Suddenly an otherwise peaceful scene might be interrupted by a peregrine falcon or merlin, diving into a flock of waders and flying off with a tasty morsel.

At Far Arnside caravan park bird tables and feeders attract nuthatch, marsh tit, bullfinch, chaffinch, robin, dunnock, great spotted woodpecker, blackbird and song thrush. However, this live bait may occasionally prove irresistible to a patrolling sparrowhawk. Here also rather curious roe deer come out of the woodlands to encroach into the residents' neat little gardens and cause mayhem.

Marsh tit. *Peter Smith*

Heathwaite and Arnside Knott, with its wooded slopes and limestone screes, comprise a botanically rich area and are protected by the National Trust. The Knott is the haunt of the raven, carrion crow, jackdaw, jay, kestrel, buzzard, mistle thrush, warblers, goldcrest, tree creeper, nuthatch, and the green and great spotted woodpecker.

Jay. *Peter Smith*

Bullfinch. *Peter Smith*

Arnside Knott's weather-beaten juniper scrub and gnarled yew trees have withstood the passage of time over hundreds of years and the views from the summit are superb. Arnside Knott is also renowned for its diverse mixture of southern and northern species at the edge of their range, with a profusion of traveller's joy or old man's beard and the extremely localised spiked speedwell. In the woods there are colonies of the southern wood ant.

The slopes rising to the summit of the Knott are endowed with blue moor grass, which is the food plant of an isolated but thriving colony of the Scotch Argus butterfly.

Other butterflies that may be encountered are the brimstone, wall brown, speckled wood, red admiral, peacock, comma, painted lady, large, small and green veined white, meadow brown, orange tip and small tortoiseshell. In summer the common lizard may be seen on the paths and limestone where it is quite at home enjoying a spot of sunbathing! Mammals include roe deer, brown hare, rabbit, stoat and weasel. It is unfortunate that the native red squirrel population has been superseded by the invasive and all-pervading grey squirrel throughout the AONB. Flocks of jackdaws are predominant in the urban setting at Arnside and nest in local quarries

During August you might find one or two specimens of the rare Scotch Argus on the summit of Arnside Knott, its only English haunt. *David Hindle*

The lovely peacock butterfly is a gem to see in early spring. *David Hindle*

and sometimes chimney pots! Nowadays that Asiatic invader of the 1960s, the collared dove, is well established at Arnside and seems to call incessantly, making a good alarm clock!

Walk 3: 'Welcome to Grange, for a walk along the Prom'

There is plenty to see and do in this very attractive Edwardian resort. To enjoy a relaxing stroll and observe some of the birds of Morecambe Bay, simply gain the promenade from the railway station and walk west along the full length of the prom to the site of the old swimming bath. Return to the railway station by the same route and divert to see more of Grange and the interesting captive waterfowl collection in the park.

Edwardian Grange was known as the 'Torquay of the North'. The promenade was built in 1904 and is now more than a mile long, and traffic-free. The ornamental gardens and pond were made on a reclaimed salt marsh, and today are the haunt of various species of interesting captive wildfowl. Close by there is a terrace of period shops and cafes. In 1932 an outdoor swimming pool was built on the seafront, but it closed in 1993 and has remained in a derelict condition ever since.

Depending on the state of the tide good views can be obtained of the waders and wildfowl of Morecambe Bay from Grange promenade. As the tide flows check the movements of flocks of oystercatchers, curlews, dunlins, knots and redshanks flying from the sands to high-tide roosts. At the same time look out for a peregrine falcon launching a sudden attack on the wader flocks. Wildfowl will sit out the tide, especially on calm days, with large numbers of wigeon, shelduck, pintail and mallard congregating on the water, and sentinel-like herons and cormorants standing around or fishing the channel. Look out for flocks of the white little egret, which have dramatically increased in recent years. They may now be regarded as common in the tidal creeks and estuarine habitats of Morecambe Bay, whereas 30 years ago it was a red letter day to see one.

Knots at the water's edge. *Peter Smith*

A peregrine falcon searching for prey. *Peter Smith*

Oystercatcher. *Peter Smith*

Dunlin. *Peter Smith*

Little egret. *Geoff Carefoot*

Walk 4: Roose station for Roa Island – coastal scenery, birds and railway heritage

This walk starts at Roose railway station and finishes at Roa Island.

Distance: 7 kilometres (one way)
Time: 5 hours
Grade: Easy
General: There are toilet and refreshment facilities at Rampside and Roa Island.
Directions: Study the bus and train timetables, as this walk utilises public transport – outward by train to Barrow, returning by bus from Roa Island to either Roose, Ulverston or Barrow railway station. The walk starts at Barrow Town Hall. Walk the short distance along Duke Street to Morrison's supermarket, turning right at the end of the building and left along the path fronting Buccleuch Dock. Turn right along Cavendish Dock Road, passing the main entrance to the port, then sharp left along a permitted path. Continue along this path, with Cavendish Dock on your left, and turn right at the next junction. Turn right along 'Greenway', passing the onshore gas terminal and Westfield Point to Rampside. Ahead is the site of Rampside railway station and the road causeway connecting with Roa Island, marking the end of the walk.

At the tip of the Furness peninsula lie the village of Rampside and four small islands – Roa Island, Piel Island, Sheep Island and Foulney Island. All are situated between mainland Furness and the southern tip of Walney Island. Foulney Island is attached to the Roa Island causeway by its own causeway. Records from Furness Abbey show that there was an abbey farm or grange nearby, known as Rameshede (Rampside), which was known as the grange with the fishery. Furness Abbey owned Piel, which, rather confusingly, was known as Foudrey or Fotheray, and may also have owned Foulney. Although Foulney has long been known as a bird island, the earliest bird records come from the 1840s when roseate and common terns nested in roughly equal numbers, and little and Arctic terns were also present.

The Furness Railway originally built its branch line in an almost straight line linking Barrow with Roa Island to ship out slate and iron ore. The causeway to Roa Island was built by John Abel Smith during the Victorian era, and he was also responsible for the construction of the pier on Roa Island and implementing the steamship service across the bay to Fleetwood. In 1852 the whole undertaking was sold to the Furness Railway Company. The railway preceded the road across the causeway, and the line survived until 1936, when the branch was closed. There was one intermediate station at Rampside, which was situated near the commencement of the causeway.

Cumbria's 'Greenway,' part of the Cumbria Coastal Way, leads from its industrial shipbuilding heartland at Cavendish Dock along the course of the old Furness Railway line, past Barrow onshore gas terminal to the village of Rampside.

In the past Cavendish Dock has been good for birdwatching, though perhaps not during recent years. It still attracts waterfowl and waders, terns, gulls and some rarities. Post-breeding dispersal leads to increased numbers of coot in autumn and winter, when great crested grebe are commonly seen.

Typically all ducks of the male gender are distinctively colourful, particularly the red-breasted merganser that may be present. In winter look out for scattered groups of diving ducks including the goldeneye, tufted duck, pochard and occasionally the long-tailed duck. As distinct from the diving ducks, surface-feeding ducks such as the wigeon, teal, mallard and shoveler may also be observed in flocks on the open water.

Seasonal passage and storms have produced the Slavonian red-necked and black-necked grebe, red-throated and black-throated, great northern diver, and occasionally the black tern and little gull. Over the years a distinguished cast of rarities has included the pectoral sandpiper, spotted sandpiper, lesser yellowlegs, white-winged black tern, woodlark, water pipit and Lapland bunting.

View the mudflats at Roosecote Sands on a rising tide from the causeway that runs along the southern side of the dock. This is an important site for wildfowl and waders, and in winter flocks of eider, wigeon, mallard, teal and shelduck occur at high tide. Feeding flocks of dunlin, knot, redshank, curlew, oystercatcher and golden plover move to the salt marsh at high tide. The little egret is one species that has considerably expanded its range in England, and nowadays small flocks may be seen in many suitable localities including Roosecote Sands, with its coastal creeks and pools.

Passage migrants such as the whimbrel and greenshank may be seen during spring and autumn passage, while opportunistic peregrines, merlins and sparrowhawks may be seen pursuing the wader flocks and smaller birds. Almost anywhere on this walk is a good place to see the resident stonechat, song thrush, kestrel, linnet and goldfinch. Passage migrants include white

Stock dove. *Geoff Carefoot*

wagtails and wheatears. During May the profusions of flowering gorse and luxuriant hawthorn also attracts the whitethroat, lesser whitethroat, blackcap, willow warbler and chiffchaff.

The onshore gas terminal close to Westfield Point is expected to process gas throughout the 40-year life of the Morecambe Bay gas field. The terminal is landscaped with several thousand trees, shrubs and ponds fringed with reeds and willow and is visible from a nature trail,

which is well worth a diversionary walk from the 'Greenway', where sedge warblers may be encountered. Check the extensive cover and hedgerows for sheltering migrants in spring and autumn. In fields close to Westfield Point there are several dykes with reedy areas and a pool where snipe may be seen feeding before flying off with their characteristic zigzag flight and harsh 'ketsch' calls. The pool is the haunt of the mute swan, coot, moorhen, wigeon, teal, snipe, redshank and reed bunting. At Rampside check the mudflats for small parties of wintering brent geese.

The final section of the walk crosses the causeway linking the Furness peninsula with Roa Island. The high road embankment affords good views of the channel separating

Arctic terns. *Peter Smith*

Brent goose. *Geoff Carefoot*

Walney Island, with its landmark white lighthouse, and Piel Island with its ruined castle.

In spring and summer a variety of terns may be seen fishing in the channel, including little, common, sandwich and Arctic terns together with migrating whimbrel during late April and May. Other regular species include the curlew, bar-tailed godwit, knot, grey plover, turnstone, dunlin, oystercatcher, eider and shelduck. During the passage period numbers of sanderling and ringed plover occur, with the largest numbers in late May; these are birds bound for their breeding areas in Northern Europe.

If time permits, do not forget to survey Roa Island to discover traces of railway archaeology, and make contact with the ferryman to explore Piel Island. It is possible to reach the castle and the King of Piel, who is known to frequent the Ship Inn, by contacting the ferryman. After partaking of a jar or two of the local brew and meeting mine host, the King, in his usual haunt, your day's list of birds should increase tenfold!

Eider. *Geoff Carefoot*

Turnstone. *Geoff Carefoot*

A flock of redshank. *Peter Smith*

Walk 5: 'Green Road – alight here for Swinside stone circle'

Grid ref: SD190840
Distance: 7 Kilometers
Time: Allow 5 hours
Grade: Easy to moderate
General: Nearest refreshment and toilet facilities are at Broughton and Millom.
Directions: Swinside stone circle is located about 7 kilometres north of Millom and can be reached by alighting from the train at Green Road Halt and walking right towards Broughton-in-Furness along the A5093. At the junction with a country lane to Broadgate, turn left and proceed to Crag Hall Farm. From the farm walk along a rough track for 2¼km (1¼ miles) uphill towards Swinside Farm, where the megalithic ring of stones lies to the right of the path.

On this walk a variety of flora and fauna may be observed in any of the scattered woodlands lining the valley, while walking to and from the little-visited stone circle, which is actually one of the finest in Britain. Buzzards are commonly seen soaring and mewing over their natural domain. In this remote area of Cumbria look and listen for a variety of birds in their natural habitat. In spring and summer there may be opportunities to observe the green and great spotted woodpecker, chiffchaff, blackcap, willow warbler, tree creeper, redstart, nuthatch and titmouse. Spotted flycatchers can also be seen darting out from cover to catch, as their name suggests, flies.

Spotted flycatcher with prey. *Peter Smith*

Blue tit. *Peter Smith*

Tree creeper. *Peter Smith*

Swinside stone circle has 55 stones, although when originally constructed there probably would have been around 60, and they are up to 3 metres (10 feet) high. Archaeological investigation into the monument began in the early 20th century, with an excavation taking place in 1901. The circle dates from the Neolithic period and its entrance/exit on the south-eastern side seems to line up with the midwinter sunset, and is defined by the inclusion of two outer portal stones. The circle's other name, Sunkenkirk, comes from the legend that attempts to build a church were thwarted by the Devil, who kept pulling it down. Constructed from local slate, the ring has a diameter of about 93ft 8in (26.8 metres).

Walk 6: 'Millom – change here for Hodbarrow Nature Reserve and industrial archaeology'

This walk starts and finishes at Millom railway station.
Distance: 7 kilometres
Time: 4 hours
Grade: Easy
General: Toilet and refreshment facilities are available at Millom. A Tourist Information Office is located at Millom railway station. It is preferable to do the walk on an incoming tide of at least 9 metres in order to obtain closer views of wildfowl and waders, both on the marshes and in the channels.
Directions: From Millom railway station turn left into Devonshire Road towards the prominent landmark of St George's church steeple on the right. After the town centre square, turn left into St George's Terrace and right into Lapstone Road, heading for Newton Street at its junction with Furness Street. Ahead lies the site of the Iron Works Nature Reserve and interpretative boards direct you to the former harbour at Borwick Rails. At the old pier there keep right to join the Cumbria Coastal Way. Walk across Hodbarrow Mains and over the headland at Hodbarrow Point to the RSPB nature reserve. Take a right-hand track

Megalithic specialist Aubrey Bud called Swinside 'the loveliest of all the circles' in north-western Europe, and it is well worth a visit. It is 5 miles north of Millom and may be reached by following walk No 5. *Neal Hardy*

that leads away from the Cumbria Coastal Way through the old mining area. Skirt the reserve before turning right onto Mainsgate Road and return to Millom station.

Millom Iron Works was once the town's principal employer until closure in 1968. Nowadays, the town is transferring its allegiance from its industrial past to tourism, including the provision of facilities for observing wildlife and birdwatching, and this walk takes in two nature reserves. The local museum has a definite focus on the railway and the mining industry; it occupies rooms at Millom railway station and is well worth a visit. Millom's most famous son is the Lakeland poet and author Norman Nicholson; we pass by No 14 St George's Terrace, his former home, where a blue plaque commemorates his life.

The Iron Works Local Nature Reserve and Borwick Rails pier demonstrate how land reclamation of a former major industrial site can be put to excellent use and enhance biodiversity. The harbour area provides excellent views of the estuary across to Dunnerholme, Sandscale and Walney Island, all set against a backdrop of the hills of the Furness peninsula and the mountains of south and west Cumbria. The site has reverted to nature and plant communities have developed on the slag

and disturbed ground, typically represented by bee orchids and yellow wort, while the grasslands host several species of butterfly. Today the old harbour at Borwick Rails plays host to birds rather than the Victorian sailing ships that once plied their trade and about which my old grandma enthused.

An Arctic tern in flight. *Peter Smith*

A close-up of the common tern. *Geoff Carefoot*

Why not have lunch at the top of the slag heap? There are worse places! Indeed, I personally have a vivid memory of the legendary place for birds that was the Freckleton sewage farm during the Swinging Sixties! Moving on, if you have planned it right by now the tide will have

started to ebb and there will be both water and exposed mud. In spring expect to see both the smallest (little tern) and largest (sandwich tern) members of the tern family, as well as the occasional more common Arctic tern, often humorously known as 'comic terns' or, perhaps more elegantly, 'sea swallows'. Up to four species of tern may be seen flying to and from the breeding colony at Hodbarrow.

The Iron Works Reserve attracts rock pipit, meadow pipit, stonechat and skylark. The Duddon estuary is the haunt of the greenshank, curlew, oystercatcher, lapwing, dunlin, red-breasted merganser, mallard, pintail, goldeneye, teal, wigeon, eider, great crested grebe, cormorant, heron and red-throated diver, as well as the little,

Sandwich, Arctic and common tern. Certain sea birds, including the gannet, guillemot and razorbill, are sometimes seen further out to sea.

Hodbarrow Point, known locally as 'The Rocks', is good for migrants taking advantage of the diversity of small cliffs, foreshore, scrub and wetlands. The RSPB's Hodbarrow Nature Reserve is the flooded site of the former iron ore mine and is enclosed by a sea wall built more than 100 years ago. Most of the industrial archaeology was removed in the 1970s and 1980s, but two lighthouse towers and the walls of a windmill remain. Near the stump of the old windmill the cliffs at Hodbarrow Point are worth exploring at low tide, being home to that localised but hardy maritime fern, the sea spleenwort. Botanically the inner part of the sea wall is very interesting

with many common limestone plants, including dark red helleborine, bloody cranesbill and pyramidal orchid. In June

Ringed plover. *Peter Smith*

Sandwich tern. *Both Geoff Carefoot*

Little tern. *Geoff Carefoot*

and early July the area of open ground to the east of the large lagoon is greatly enhanced by colonies of northern marsh, pyramidal and bee orchids.

Several species of butterfly are attracted to the reserve. The red admiral, small tortoiseshell, painted lady, dark green fritillary and grayling butterfly all add a touch of colour as they flit around their favoured food plants. Rare amphibians are represented by natterjack toads, engaging creatures that breed in several pools where dragonflies hawk over the water during the summer months looking to lay their eggs. At high tide do not be too surprised to find an Atlantic grey seal watching you, or maybe even a common seal. The latter is badly named, for it is not nearly so common as the grey seal around the British coast; its alternative name of harbour seal is perhaps preferable.

Hodbarrow Reserve is important for the passage of wildfowl and waders and as a breeding site for them, including the declining ringed plover. The reserve can be viewed while walking round it or from a hide located on the sea wall, which is open all year. The main lagoon and smaller meres are now home to many species of waterfowl, including large numbers of red-breasted mergansers and thousands of waders in autumn and winter. Of particular importance, however, is the specially protected tern colony that hosts several British species including a thriving sandwich tern colony of up to 500 pairs and the fast diminishing little tern, a real speciality of the reserve. With any luck the young birds from this colony will have fledged by the end of June and be on the wing, thus presenting a few more identification challenges.

Walk 7: Silecroft and the ascent of Black Combe

This walk starts and finishes at Silecroft railway station.
Distance: 9 kilometres
Time: Allow 4 to 5 hours
Grade: Moderate
General: Toilet and refreshment facilities are available at Silecroft.
Directions: From Silecroft station, turn right through the village and follow the main road left towards Whicham, taking the first turning right at the road junction. Walk towards Whicham church and take the first turning left along a quiet lane to the start of the climb up the south-west face of Black Combe. After passing the farm, cross a stile and follow a grassy track up through the lower slopes of the valley of Moor Gill Beck to a short steep stretch before gaining the 400-metre contour. This is the hardest bit and from here onwards the pace is more relaxing before a subsidiary peak is reached, and eventually an arrow of stones pointing right to the summit. The easiest way to descend is to retrace your steps to Whicham church.

This walk extends from Silecroft to the summit of Black Combe and provides an opportunity to see a range of upland birds.

For safety reasons do not attempt to climb Black Combe when there is low cloud or when the locals say that 'the Combe has got a cap on it today'. Be aware that east of the rounded summit there are potentially dangerous rocky slopes with high crags and screes. The isolated outcrop of Black Combe's rugged grandeur can be seen dominating the landscape to the north of Morecambe Bay; it is 600 metres high, which is just short of mountain status.

The quiet lane leading from Whicham Church to the lower slopes of Black Combe may produce linnet, blackcap, willow warbler, long-tailed tit, stonechat, meadow pipit, skylark, pied wagtail and a sadly declining population of yellowhammer and cuckoo. The ubiquitous hedgehog can turn up when least expected – I once saw one rummaging in the unspoilt hedgerow bordering the lane. The instantly recognisable call of the male cuckoo compels attention and heralds the coming of spring. The cuckoo has sadly declined in many parts of Britain. The male calls both in flight and when perched, but despite this it is often difficult to locate. When calling from a perch he has a very characteristic pose with head bowed forward, drooping wings and elevated fanned tail.

Take a walk eastwards from the trig point to enjoy a panoramic view over the crags of Black Combe's eastern buttress towards White Combe, but don't drop off the crag! This is an excellent place to enjoy the tranquillity of the mountain with a timely meal break. At the same time look out for upland raptors typically represented by peregrine, kestrel and buzzard. Short-eared owls are occasionally seen quartering the fellside. The raucous call of the raven and the familiar call of the jackdaw may

Hedgehog. *Peter Smith*

Linnet. *Peter Smith*

Peregrine falcon

Stonechat. *Peter Smith*

Short-eared owl. *Peter Smith*

often be heard in this habitat, which is shared with meadow pipit and wheatear.

To the south-west the view towards Blackpool Tower and the coastal plain of the Wyre estuary at Fleetwood extends north across Morecambe Bay to Walney Island. North thereof is the wide expanse of the Duddon estuary and the Lake District's western and central mountains and valleys. On a clear day it is possible to make out the mountains of North Wales, Dumfries & Galloway, the Isle of Man and the Irish coast.

Walk 8: 'St Bees – change for St Bees Head RSPB Reserve'

This linear walk begins at St Bees railway station and ends at Whitehaven railway station.
Distance: 9 kilometres
Time: Allow 5 to 6 hours for the complete walk
Grade: Easy to moderate
General: There are obvious dangers on the high cliff top and children need to be closely supervised. Also the cliff-top path is steep in places and there are several stiles. Toilets and refreshment facilities are to be found at St Bees and Whitehaven.
Directions: From St Bees railway station walk along the road to the shore and take the obvious cliff-top path to the north of the car park. Ascend the south headland by a steep path and continue walking north along the cliff top. Follow the path along the south head before descending to Fleswick Bay between the two headlands. From Fleswick Bay follow the coastal path onto the north headland stopping

at each of the three observation platforms. At the lighthouse you have a choice of either returning to St Bees station by the same route, or to continue along the cliff-top walk for approximately 5 kilometres to Whitehaven station. If the latter option is chosen, follow the cliff-top path north from the lighthouse on the north head past the remains of Haig Colliery to Whitehaven, where the descent to the harbour is steeply graded with steps. The railway station is situated close to the harbour at the northern end of the town centre.

The St Bees RSPB reserve is the only cliff nesting sea bird colony in the North West of England and a visit at the height of the breeding season in May and June is a unique and unforgettable experience. The red sandstone cliffs, rising to almost 300 feet, provide nesting sites for a myriad of sea birds. All species are visible from the cliff-top footpath and the best sites have three specially constructed viewing platforms allowing one to experience the constant activity and cacophony of sound (and smell) of a sea bird city at close quarters.

The sea bird inhabitants of the south head are mainly herring gulls, fulmars and razorbills. The north head has much more diversity and greater numbers. The small marshy area at the start of the cliffs holds breeding sedge warblers. Rock pipits occur right from the start, but can be difficult to spot as they flit among the rocks. The best views are usually obtained at Fleswick Bay, where they often forage on the tide line, while wheatears favour the turf and boulder walls. The gorse-dominated areas, close to Fleswick Bay allow excellent views of the stonechat, whitethroat and linnet. Little owls have also been seen in the same area, often sitting on a post, usually towards dusk.

From the top of the headland it is well worth scanning the sea as, besides the breeding sea birds, gannets regularly pass to and fro from their breeding colonies of Scar Rocks and Ailsa Craig off the Galway coast. With favourable onshore winds Manx

shearwaters and occasionally petrels and skuas may also be observed. Sandwich terns are regular, especially in spring and late summer.

For much of spring and summer the cliffs and footpath edges are alive with colour. There are drifts of scabious, thrift, sea campion and scurvy grass and plenty of gorse. Butterflies to look out for include the gatekeeper, grayling and small copper.

To many birdwatchers the highlight of a trip to St Bees is the sight of a black guillemot. St Bees Head is the only regular breeding site in England for this handsome black and white species, which favours the boulder-strewn beach of Fleswick Bay. This is the rarest of the reserve's breeding sea

birds with only around five pairs nesting. Searching through the rafts of auks floating on the water is usually successful – the dazzling white wing patches and crimson legs contrasting with the black plumage really makes it obvious. Puffins are also rare breeders at St Bees, though they can sometimes be on the sea or cliffs viewable from the RSPB observation platforms on the north head. Persevere and you might just be rewarded with views of this delightful sea bird with its bizarre multi-coloured bill.

The most impressive spectacle at St Bee's north headland is the massed ranks of guillemots occupying every suitable ledge. The density on some ledges is such

Gatekeeper butterfly. *Peter Smith*

Small copper butterfly. *Peter Smith*

Grayling butterfly. *Peter Smith*

that birds incubating the single egg appear to huddle side by side. The contrast of the sleek chocolate brown and white plumage against the red sandstone cliff coupled with the constant movement and the cacophony of sound is overall a wonderful experience. The guillemot's close relative the razorbill nests in much smaller numbers. With good views the two are easy to separate, the razorbill's heavy bill and darker body being distinctive. Razorbills nest in a crevice typically under a boulder, whereas guillemots nest on the open sheer cliff's ledges.

Kittiwakes, that most oceanic of gulls, are like puffins sadly in national decline due to a shortage of sand eels, but may still be seen at St Bees. Unlike the auks, kittiwakes build a nest on the cliffs so are never as concentrated as guillemots. The call from which the bird gets its name echoes in chorus 'kitti-wark kitti-wark' from the nesting cliffs.

Sudden disturbance of the nesting sea birds usually betrays the presence of a hunting peregrine, even though its main prey are the many feral pigeons in the area. Cormorants nest in small numbers, and are easily picked out standing around in small groups on the rocks below or flying along the bottom of the cliffs.

Fulmars, a member of the petrel family, nest in small numbers scattered along the

How many sand eels in this puffin's bill? *Geoff Carefoot*

The aptly named razorbill. *Peter Smith*

A guillemot family. *Peter Smith*

cliffs where they prefer the larger, more vegetated ledges. They are a sheer joy to watch as they soar along the cliff edge with effortless elegance. The best time to visit the reserve is certainly from May to mid-July. The first guillemots can return briefly to the cliffs around the turn of the year but numbers start to assemble at the colony in February together with many of the other species. Early in the year they often appear nervous and fly out to sea if a person or boat appears. As the season progress all species become strongly territorial. By mid-July the young guillemots are ready to leave the ledges, before they can fly – usually towards dusk they jump off the ledges with tiny wings flapping and large feet spread out, often attended by an anxious adult. Once on the water their parents locate them by their loud incessant calling and escort them out to sea.

North of the lighthouse the walk along the cliffs to Whitehaven is less birdy, with no more spectacular sea bird colonies like those concentrated south of the lighthouse. However, offshore schools of bottlenose or common dolphins may be seen anywhere from any of the cliffs throughout the walk. Keep watch also for the peregrine, kestrel, raven, numerous herring gulls and cormorants, and passerines like the willow warbler, whitethroat, rock pipit and linnet. In spring the ground flora is dominated by thrift, bluebells, red campion, greater stitchwort and several species of orchids. Any lack of birds may be compensated for by the fine views across the Irish Sea to the Isle of Man and Crifell and the Galloway Hills on the north bank of the Solway Firth.

Approaching Whitehaven the walk passes by sites of industrial archaeology associated with the coal-mining industry, and the town itself is worthy of exploration. Below the cliffs on the approach are a few relics of Saltom Pit, which once echoed to the sound of the steam winding engine and the voices of several generations of miners. Saltom Pit was England's first undersea coal mine and it took three years to sink the shaft to a depth of 146 fathoms from 1729. The coal face was 2 kilometres from the shore and miners, including children, lost their lives in Saltom's tunnels. Just imagine working as a 9-year-old at the coal face in a pitch-black tunnel far under the sea bed prior to the closure of Saltom in 1848!

A little further towards Whitehaven is the site of the King Pit shaft, which was sunk in 1750. It reached a depth of 160 fathoms and at the time was considered to be the deepest pits in the world. It goes without saying that coal mines were dangerous places to work, but a necessary evil to put food on the table. At the top of the steep slope leading down to the harbour the solitary tall ventilation shaft aptly named 'the candlestick' stands as another remnant of the coal industry. The path leading down to the harbour utilises part of the old railway trackbed, where standard-gauge coal wagons were hoisted up the Howgill rope incline between the harbour wall and Haig Colliery.

At Whitehaven today there is no trace of the old Ladysmith washery. This installation was connected to Haig Colliery to the north by a single-track railway that has now been realigned as part of the coastal walk. During the late 1960s I photographed heavily laden NCB steam-hauled freight trains working extremely hard up the steeply graded line between Haig Colliery and the Ladysmith washery. I also enjoyed footplate rides on several NCB engines along the wobbly old tracks perched high on the cliffs from Haig Pit to the washery on several earth-shattering occasions! The accompanying photographs hopefully capture the essence of the end of the coal-mining industry and industrial steam in Cumbria.

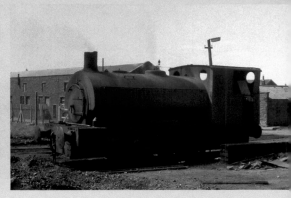

Above: The damaged workhorse *Repulse* (left) is shown in steam at Haig Colliery alongside sister engine *Revenge* in 1968. These 'Austerities' were tough, but with serious damage it is a wonder that the saddle tank still held water. Nevertheless, *Repulse* was finally withdrawn in March 1975 and almost scrapped before being moved to the Lakeside & Haverthwaite Railway for a long and challenging restoration. *David Hindle*

Right: A magnificent setting, but it looks like a hazardous environment for locomotives (and their crews). In addition to the damage seen on its sister loco *Repulse*, it looks like *Revenge* has taken a hit on the left-hand side of the cab. High on the cliffs overlooking the Irish Sea, another rake of hopper wagons is propelled by the loco as work goes on. The Haig mine workings went out under the sea here to access the coal seams. *David Hindle*

Above centre: Flanked on both sides by wooden-bodied coal wagons, and with the two pit-head winding gear towers behind, 0-6-0ST *Revenge* makes a fine sight as it shunts steel hopper wagons at Haig Colliery. Although steam working finished soon after this, the pit itself survived until 1986. *David Hindle*

Above: Another battered-looking locomotive was this 0-4-0ST, still in steam at Ladysmith washery in 1968. *David Hindle*

Augmented bus services

Visitors wishing to embark for their own grand tour of the glorious English Lake District, exploring the northern and central Lake District, should consider their itinerary and, in addition to rail travel, enquire into bus timetables. Visit the Stagecoach website for more information – with a little planning you can reach many places by bus from Workington and other bus terminals in the Lake District.

X4/X5 Workington-Cockermouth-Keswick-Penrith This service runs from Workington bus station via Cockermouth to Keswick, then continues to Penrith. Alternate hourly services serve the villages of Threlkeld, Thornthwaite, Bassenthwaite and Embleton. Walkers can use the bus to complete both linear and circular walks without the necessity of having to return to where they left their car.

Top left: The rickety railway line at Haig was precariously situated on the edge of a high cliff. *Revenge* is shown propelling its train up the steep mile-long gradient to the washery. *David Hindle*

Left: Emptying ash from *Repulse* on 11 September 1974. *Peter Fitton*

555 Lancaster-Keswick This service runs between Lancaster and Keswick via Kendal, Windermere railway station, Ambleside and Grasmere. The breathtaking route follows the Helvellyn chain to Grasmere, then to Ambleside, Windermere and beyond to Kendal. Often this ride will be by double-decker - the scenery is better from the top deck than from the back seat of a car.

78 runs from Keswick via Lodore, Grange Bridge, Rosthwaite to Seatoller (Borrowdale).

77/77A 'The Honister Rambler' is a circular seasonal bus service that operates from Easter to October in both clockwise and anti-clockwise directions taking in Portinscale, Catbells, Grange, Seatoller, Honister Slate Mine, Buttermere, Lorton and Whinlatter Forest. You can step on a bus to explore the beauty of Borrowdale or cross the Honister Pass for the breathtaking views of Buttermere and Crummock Water, returning to Keswick through the gentle Vale of Lorton and over the Whinlatter Pass with its Visitor Centre and osprey CCTV screens. The osprey outdoor viewpoint above Mirehouse is only a few minutes bus ride from Keswick.

Bibliography

Primary sources – Lancashire Archives

LBP/60/24 – Furness Railway Bill, 1894

DDCA 22/1810 – Re signal box

DDCACC12005 – Lease to run Furness Abbey and adjacent land

DDCA/12005/6697A – Stank branch

DDCA/ACC12005/Box 31 – Large bundle of correspondence and other documents relating to the Furness Railway

DDCA/ACC12005/Box 34/382 – Legal documents re Sir James Ramsden

DDCA/ACC12005/Box 30/405 – Notice re Furness Railway and Piel Harbour

QSP4732/682 – Byelaws re regulation of traffic, Barrow harbour and docks

QDP/1/21 – Extension of Furness Railway to Broughton

PDR 201 – Extension of Furness Railway, Ulverston to Lancaster.

DDX 162/63/25 – Plan of route of Arnside-Hincaster branch

Secondary sources

Andrews, M. *The Furness Railway in and around Barrow* (Cumbrian Railways Association, 2003)

Andrews & Holne, G. *The Coniston Railway* (Cumbrian Railways Association, 2005)

Arman, Brian *The H. L. Hopwood Collection, 1901-1926, Part 2: The Furness Railway at Barrow in 1902* (Rly Archive, 2008)

Aslett, A. *English Lakeland: Furness Railway* (W. Holmes Ltd, Ulverston, 1916)

Bradshaw, G. *Railway Guide* (first published in 1863)

Davey, C. R. *Reflections of the Furness Railway* (Lakeland Heritage Books, 1984)

Davies, W. J. K. *The Ravenglass & Eskdale Railway* (David & Charles, 1981)

Grosse, P. *The railways of Carnforth town and its iron works* (Barrai Books, 2014)

Heavyside, T. *Lancashire & Cumberland's Last Days of Colliery Steam* (Stenlake, 2007)

Hindle, D. J. *Twice Nightly* (Carnegie Publishing, 1999)
All Stations to Longridge (Amberley Publishing, 2010)
Preston Planes, Trains, Tramcars and Ships (Amberley Publishing 2015)

Hindle, D. J. & Wilson, J. *Birdwatching walks around Morecambe Bay* (Carnegie Publishing 2007)
Birdwatching Walks in the Lake District (Carnegie Publishing 2010)

Joy, D. *Regional History of the Railways of Great Britain* (David and Charles)
Cumbrian Coast Railways (Dalesman Publishing Company, 1968)

McGowan, Gradon *Furness Railway: Its rise and development 1846-1923* (1946)

Marshall, J. *Lancashire & Yorkshire Railway* (David & Charles, 1969)

Mather, D. *Exploring the Lake District with the Furness Railway Tours* (Silver Link Publishing, 2015)

Melville, J & Hobbs *Early Railway History in Furness* (Cumberland & Westmorland Antiquarian & Archaeological Society, 1951)

Norman K. J. *Railway Heritage: The Furness Railway* (Silver Link Publishing, 1994)
The Furness Railway: Volumes 1 & 2 (Silver Link Publishing, 1994 and 2001)

Western, R. *The Coniston Railway* (Oakwood Press, 2007)
The Cockermouth, Keswick & Penrith Railway (Oakwood Press, 2007)

Index